D1613550

St. Thomas More: Action and Contemplation

Sir Thomas More, by Hans Holbein

St. Thomas More: Action and Contemplation

PROCEEDINGS OF THE SYMPOSIUM
HELD AT ST. JOHN'S UNIVERSITY,
OCTOBER 9–10, 1970

Edited, with an Introduction,
by Richard S. Sylvester

YALE UNIVERSITY PRESS
FOR ST. JOHN'S UNIVERSITY:
NEW HAVEN AND LONDON: 1972

Library of Congress catalog card number: 77-179478
International standard book number: 0-300-01507-0

Designed by Sally Sullivan
and set in Linotype Baskerville type.
Printed in the United States of America by
Vail-Ballou Press, Inc., Binghamton, N.Y.

Distributed in Great Britain, Europe, and Africa by
Yale University Press, Ltd., London; in Canada by
McGill-Queen's University Press, Montreal; in Latin America
by Kaiman & Polon, Inc., New York City; in India by UBS Publishers'
Distributors Pvt., Ltd., Delhi; in Japan by John
Weatherhill, Inc., Tokyo.

CONTENTS

FOREWORD

The Anglo-American Associates is most grateful to St. John's University both for its invitation to sponsor the St. Thomas More Symposium on its campus and for the extremely generous subsidy that made possible the assembling of so distinguished a company of scholars. This first international conference held under the aegis of the Anglo-American Associates owed its extraordinary success in large part to the University.

Tribute must also be paid to Professor Richard S. Sylvester, General Editor of the great Yale Edition of the Works of St. Thomas More, who arranged the program and masterminded the proceedings with consummate imagination and skill.

Ruth Emery
Executive Secretary
Anglo-American Associates

ACKNOWLEDGMENTS

It is with the deepest sense of gratitude that I take this opportunity to thank St. John's University for making possible the St. Thomas More Symposium which convened at its Jamaica, New York, campus on October 9 and 10, 1970. If we were, indeed, the last of a number of scholarly conferences held at the University as it celebrated its centennial year, nevertheless the warm words of welcome extended to us by the President of the University, the Very Reverend Joseph T. Cahill, made all of us feel that such generous hospitality was part of a fine tradition which would continue to flourish.

When President Cahill spoke on Friday afternoon, he climaxed a brief degree-granting ceremony which honored Dr. Ruth Emery of Rutgers University and Dr. Ross J. S. Hoffman of Fordham University. To Professor Emery in particular must go much of the credit for the original planning of the Symposium. It was she, together with J. Jean Hecht of Columbia University, who, if I may so put it, first 'had the inspiration' to hold such a conference; and it was their devoted attention to many a small detail which kept our preparations current during the year and one half preceding our meetings. From our first planning session in March 1969 we had the firm support and careful guidance of Professor Edward T. Fagan of the St. John's University

School of Law, where Thomas More has long had a special place of honor. Joining with Professor Fagan was Professor Gaetano L. Vincitorio of the Department of History, whose efficiency, assiduity, and imaginative handling of manifold problems contributed so greatly to the success of the Symposium. His name must stand here for all of those members of the arrangements committee who never failed to lend a hand where it was most needed. Finally, both program and arrangement committees were always able to draw on the unflagging energies of the Reverend Joseph I. Dirvin, Vice President for University Relations; it was fittingly Father Dirvin, Director of the Centennial Year Program, who opened our first session with a reading of More's great Tower prayer, "Give me thy grace, good Lord."

Our thanks go out also to David R. Watkins, Director of Libraries at Brandeis University, who, with the expert aid of R. J. Schoeck, organized the fine exhibition of sixteenth-century law books that graced the De Andreis Gallery in which our meetings took place. William Gillard, Librarian at St. John's made all his facilities available to us for the exhibition; the books themselves were loaned from the Beinecke Rare Book Library of Yale University where Miss Marjorie Wynne's assistance, here as on many other occasions, was deeply appreciated. The Yale University Press, represented by Mrs. Jennifer R. Alkire, displayed its sixteenth-century publications at a much-frequented table. Mrs. Alkire's contribution to the symposium, and that of the Yale Press, began then; but, as the present volume itself indicates, they have continued to play their part in preserving the memory of our two days at St. John's.

Our chairmen, commentators and lecturers speak for themselves in the pages that follow. During our sessions we were blessed with an audience which, again and again, demonstrated both its warm interest in and its sensitive knowledge of Saint Thomas More. To them, and to our sponsors, this volume is dedicated.

Richard S. Sylvester
Yale University
December 24, 1970

LIST OF SHORT TITLES

CW	*The Yale Edition of the Complete Works of St. Thomas More,* vol. 2 *(Richard III),* 1963; vol. 4 *(Utopia),* 1965; vol. 5 *(Responsio ad Lutherum),* 1969. Yale University Press, New Haven and London.
EW	*The Workes of Sir Thomas More Knyght . . . in the English Tonge.* London, 1557.
LP	*Letters and Papers Foreign and Domestic of the Reign of Henry VIII,* ed. J. S. Brewer, J. Gairdner, and R. Brodie, 21 vols. London, 1862–1932.
SL	*St. Thomas More: Selected Letters,* ed. E. F. Rogers. New Haven, 1961.
Allen	*Opus Epistolarum Des. Erasmi Roterodami,* ed. P. S. Allen, H. M. Allen, et al., 12 vols. Oxford, 1906–58.
Chambers	R. W. Chambers, *Thomas More.* London, 1935.
Rogers	E. F. Rogers, ed., *The Correspondence of Sir Thomas More.* Princeton, 1947.
Roper	*The Lyfe of Sir Thomas More, knighte,* ed. E. V. Hitchcock. London, 1935. A modern spelling version is available in *Two Early Tudor Lives,* ed. R. S. Sylvester and D. P. Harding. New Haven, 1962.

Unless otherwise noted, quotations from sixteenth-century texts are given in modern spelling.

INTRODUCTION

We began, as the brochures announcing the symposium indicated, not very far from Utopia. One might say, indeed, that Utopia was never very distant from our discussions;— how could it be, given the admirable location (Grand Central and Utopia Parkways), at which our sessions took place? Curiously enough, however, as several commentators remarked towards the end of our sessions, our main speakers tended to tack away from More's masterpiece of 1516 rather than to steer directly into its comfortable-seeming harbor. There was, as gradually emerged, more than mere seamanship involved in these maneuvers. The utopians, one recalls, had the treacherous habit of shifting landmarks in their bay so that potential enemies might come to grief.[1] Professor Schoeck's comment on this point was particularly valuable: "There is a real danger in extracting little items from *Utopia* in order to illustrate More's life and beliefs." The work is a fiction and the details of life in Utopian society should be analyzed in their artistic context. Equally pertinent was Father Marc'hadour's later remark: "One may use More's other works to throw light on the *Utopia;* the reverse procedure *is not* the one which I have been using." Several of our speakers and commentators had in fact

1. *CW 4,* 110: "His in diuersa translatis loca, hostium quam libet numerosam classem facile in perniciem traherent."

written on *Utopia* in other contexts,[2] and it is also true that
Professor Elton built his paper around the dilemma proposed in Book I of *Utopia*—can a good man be of any real
use to an indifferent, much less a bad, king if he decides to
serve him as a councillor?

Thus we constantly hovered near the approaches to
Utopia, but we never zeroed in on the central issues posed
by that seminal work. That this was so is due in part to the
immense amount of scholarly interest which *Utopia,* often
treated *in vacuo,* has excited during the present century.[3]
We were aiming, as the title of this volume indicates, at
other goals, trying not so much to see Thomas More in and
through his masterpiece, as to open up new points of view
and new topics for research in the relatively neglected areas
of his life and work that both preceded and followed the
appearance of *Utopia* itself. During, roughly, the last fifteen
years, More scholarship has become increasingly aware of
the complexity of its subject. Our "Man for All Seasons" can
be studied in terms of his legal career; he can be viewed as
a diplomat and councillor. Since the rediscovery of his
Tower Prayer Book,[4] his final meditations can be newly
evaluated, a study which enlarges our view of his spiritu-

2. See, for example, R. J. Schoeck, " 'A Nursery of Correct and
Useful Institutions': On Reading More's *Utopia* as Dialogue," *Moreana*
22 (1969): 19–32, and R. S. Sylvester, "Si Hythlodaeo Credimus:
Vision and Revision in Thomas More's *Utopia,*" *Soundings* (formerly
The Christian Scholar) 51 (1968): 272–89.

3. Much previous scholarship on *Utopia* is summed up in the Yale
Edition (*CW 4*), ed. by E. Surtz and J. H. Hexter. Particularly valuable
is H. S. Herbrüggen, *Utopie und Anti-Utopie* (Bochum-Langendreer,
1960). For the influence of More's work, see J. Max Patrick, "Utopias
and Dystopias, 1500–1750," in *St. Thomas More: A Preliminary Bibliography,* ed. R. W. Gibson and J. Max Patrick (New Haven, 1961),
pp. 291–412. A provocative recent discussion is Robbin S. Johnson's
More's Utopia, Ideal and Illusion (New Haven, 1969).

4. See Louis L. Martz and Richard S. Sylvester, eds., *Thomas More's
Prayer Book* (New Haven, 1969).

ality as it developed in the early years of his life. We have, moreover, been blessed with a variety of new materials, especially the holograph manuscript of the *Expositio Passionis*[5] and a number of new letters.[6] In addition, Professor Margaret Hastings' work promises soon to give us an account of More's years as Chancellor of the Duchy of Lancaster (1525–29), and similar studies will undoubtably lead to a reassessment of his judicial activities as lord chancellor.[7]

We thus committed ourselves, with some deliberation, to a reassessment of More as he stands now, almost five hundred years after his birth. Behind each speaker, as he presented his paper, was the Holbein portrait of More, brooding over the proceedings. One says "brooding" advisedly, for, as Professor Martz noted toward the end of our third session, the portrait does indeed have a certain grim quality to it. Perhaps the More of late 1526 or early 1527 [8] already foresaw the beleaguered and embattled position which he was to occupy during the last eight years of his life. Beneath the robes of state is the hair shirt. More was not, Professor Martz continued, a "conventional saint," but then no saint is conventional. They are all complex, yet

5. For an account of this manuscript (now in Valencia at the College of Corpus Christi), see Geoffrey Bullough, "More in Valencia," *The Tablet* 217 (Dec. 21, 1963): 1379–80, and Clarence Miller, "The Holograph of More's *Expositio Passionis*," *Moreana* 15–16 (1967): 372–79. The manuscript, edited by Professor Miller, will be published in facsimile as vol. 13, part 2 of the Yale edition of More's works.

6. See H. S. Herbrüggen, ed., *Sir Thomas More, Neue Briefe* (Münster, 1966). Herbrüggen's extensive introduction places the letters firmly in their historical and humanistic context.

7. Most suggestive in this regard, and in many ways a companion piece to Professor Elton's lecture in this volume, is his "More and the Opposition to Henry VIII," *Moreana* 15–16 (1967): 285–303.

8. For a discussion of the date of the portrait (reproduced in this volume as a frontispiece), see G. Marc'hadour, *L'Univers de Thomas More* (Paris, 1963), pp. 37–38.

they achieve a special kind of spiritual concentration which both includes and transcends all those human failings to which they, like other men, are prone.

As our sessions developed we were often reminded of More's frailty. This in itself was significant, for all too frequently the tradition of More hagiography, from Roper on, has tended to neglect those aspects of his career which did not directly contribute to his later canonization. Not everyone, perhaps, would agree with Professor Elton that "we must get at the man inside the plaster statue," but all should be grateful for the new biographical data which he now so systematically provides. Elton's emphasis on the "routine" aspect of More's career before 1529 led to a lively round of comments. Just how effective were More's efforts to influence Henry VIII? Father Marc'hadour, declining to "wrestle" with Professor Elton, nevertheless noted that perhaps too much holiness was imputed to More's motivation in earlier studies; now, however, we may run the risk of taking away too much from him. Curiously enough, R. W. Chambers' much-acclaimed biography was also downgraded. It became clear, as one of our commentators remarked, that "More did not die for the League of Nations." [9]

We had hoped, as our provisional title for the symposium suggested ("St. Thomas More: The Man and His Work"), to throw new light on the problems which More's career and writings raise. Professor Schoeck's opening paper did indeed, as the ensuing discussion showed, open up a variety of seminal topics. Schoeck placed More firmly in the context of his times as a practicing lawyer who also developed a considerable knowledge of the canon law. Readers of the present volume will be grateful for his expanded documentation of the Hunne case, reviewed by More at several points in his later polemical writings. Our commentators,

9. Professor Dickens, referring to a remark made to him by Dom David Knowles.

however, were immediately attracted by the various interpretations proposed by Professor Schoeck of More's trial
and his conduct during it. It was here, quite early in our
discussions, that we engaged several topics which were to
echo and re-echo in our later sessions.

The trial itself raises several perplexing problems.[10]
Justice Fitzjames' words, "If the act of Parliament be not
unlawful, then is not the indictment in my conscience
insufficient," [11] raise, as Elton pointed out, a purely technical question. Does the indictment answer in all details the
form which is proper for such documents? In all probability,
it did, but the Treason Trial Act of 1534, under which
More was tried, was very rarely used in cases of treason.
More offenders suffered under the Treason Act of 1536,
which tends to make More's own case somewhat anomalous.
Roper's narrative obscures that fact that four counts were
brought against More, though only one, as the case developed, was made the main issue.[12] Normally, two witnesses
were required in an indictment for treason; yet the condemnation of More depended on the evidence of only one
(Richard Rich). Moreover, Rich's account of his interview
with More in the Tower (as recorded in the indictment)
conflicts with the words recorded in Roper's narrative. We
can be sure, however, that the term "maliciously," so
strongly stressed by More, was not fundamental as far as
the jury was concerned. All such acts, in their eyes, were to

10. See the discussion by J. Duncan M. Derrett, "The Trial of Sir
Thomas More," *English Historical Review* 79 (1964): 449–77, and also
his "Neglected Versions of the Contemporary Account of the Trial of
Sir Thomas More," *Bulletin of the Institute of Historical Research* 33
(1960): 202–23.

11. Roper, p. 95.

12. The question of Roper's reliability as a reporter prompted some
spirited comment. He was not, most probably, at the trial himself; but
he was a trained lawyer and he does say that he relied directly on the
eye-witness account of Sir Richard Heywood, and others, themselves
present at the trial (Roper, p. 96).

be construed as "malicious." More's own conduct at the trial can best be understood as an accomplished lawyer's effort to be cast out of the indictment. He was, in Elton's words, "a lawyer using the devices of the law and the normal processes of the treason trial, rather than the philosopher or spiritual man expressing his deepest beliefs. He does that when it is all over, and instead of making a plea in extenuation and for mercy, which is usual after sentence, he then lets go and tells us all about his real feelings. That is the only stage in the whole trial when More did not behave like an experienced lawyer on trial for his life."

If More's view of the common law, under which he was tried, was thus that of the professional, the same could not necessarily be said of his attitude toward canon law. Opinion here divided sharply and had wide-ranging implications. Professor Kuttner noted the unusual phrase "received in England," remarking that the very idea that canon law could possibly not be received in England was in itself an abrupt departure from the medieval view. Previously there was no suggestion that canon law had not been received, but the new "dispensation" is suggestive of the way in which ecclesiastical prerogative is under attack during More's lifetime. And what of More himself? How did he conceive of canon law? Professor Marius' work as editor of More's *Confutation* enriched his reflections on this subject. For More, "law, like revelation, was an experience." It is something that develops through history. No individual decretal has ultimate authority, but all combine to present a unified *corpus,* which can itself be subject to future change. This element of the experiential, the historical, the personal, in More's thought and works, was to be a continuing theme in our later sessions.

Coupled with the question of More's conduct during his trial (first raised by Professor Schoeck) was the apparently remarkable phenomenon of his silence under interrogation before his last speech. It soon became evident that this silence covered a multitude of More's virtues (or potential sins). On the one hand, he could not swear to the royal supremacy—to do so would violate his conscience; on the other, he could not, by prematurely expressing his real views, seek his own death. And More did feel deeply, as Professor Miller noted, the obligation to avoid seeking his own death, if this were at all possible. He would not be presumptuous, would not deliberately aim at martyrdom. Silence was surely no guarantee of safety, and More himself never believed that he was being tried for his silence. To stipulate too precisely on this point is to overlook the fact that silence in such matters is generally construed as refusal. More had, as he admitted, entertained the possibility of hypothetical utterance; [13] he would not let such conversations (the key one was with Rich) be allowed as testimony in his trial.

Working through our debate over More's silence were a number of questions about his final (*post silentium*) speech. When he affirmed his allegiance to the "common corps of Christendom," citing a realm larger than England as the repository of his deepest beliefs, did he really mean to assert that he was willing to suffer for papal hegemony? The point is doubtful. Papal infallibility was never a cardinal element in More's beliefs. As Professor Headley so aptly phrased it,[14] More thought of the papacy as a "*locus,* a center of gravity," when he wrote in defense of Henry VIII against Luther in 1523. The central question remained: did More's views undergo any radical change before he embarked on his polemical works? As Headley put it, "Did More come to conciliarism gradually, reaching

13. For More's "putting of cases" with Rich during their interview in the Tower, see Roper, pp. 85–86 and the discussion by E. E. Reynolds, *The Trial of St. Thomas More* (New York, 1964), pp. 68–69 and 106f.
14. Cf. *CW* 5, Introduction, where Headley's views are set out in full detail.

by 1532 the position (carefully delineated by Professor Marius) where he could hold that a validly called council was the final authority in spiritual matters?"

Several commentators offered other observations on the question of More's conciliarism, many of them taking as their point of departure Professor Dickens' opening statement at our Friday afternoon session. For Dickens, More's trial raised broad issues of international law and political theory. It should not be considered merely in terms of a native, common law tradition. How far was More actually going when he declared in his last speech that England was related to the rest of Christendom in the same way that the City of London was related to the realm of England? Brother Coogan noted that Erasmus' annotations of the New Testament often manifest conciliar views, and Professor Marius pointed out that More and Fisher differ radically from each other in their interpretations of key scriptural texts that could be employed to defend a doctrine of papal supremacy. Professor Schoeck helped to put the topic in a contemporary setting by reflecting on the failure of the Fifth Lateran Council (1512–17). More and his humanist friends could not but have been deeply disappointed over this abortive effort at reform.

A further question raised by Professor Dickens led directly to what became, to quote Father Marc'hadour, perhaps the "most pregnant" theme of our subsequent discussions. Did More, Dickens asked, really admit that other men besides himself possessed rights of conscience? Admittedly, More's own "case of conscience," as Professor Martz's lecture had suggested, was deeply complex. Yet it seems clear, as Marius emphasized, that More never entertained the possibility that Tyndale and Barnes, for example, were also in some sense following their own consciences. Such rebels had no rights and their beliefs were, *ipso facto,* maliciously held. Professor Kuttner reminded the audience that "conscience" should be viewed here in its late medieval context where ethical speculation had never reached firm conclusions concerning the right of an heretical conscience.

Cromwell himself had of course posed this very problem to More; [15] and Margaret Roper in her letter to Alice Alington, which Professor Martz so deftly analyzed in his lecture, wondered how her father could rest his silence on the convictions of his own conscience when so many other learned men in the kingdom had not experienced similar difficulties. While it remains true, as Miller pointed out, that More often affirmed his unwillingness to influence the conscience of others, no doubt he—like thoughtful men in any age—had ultimately to draw the line, to set limits (especially in his dealings with the reformers) on others' rights of conscience when their beliefs began to upset the received opinion of the age. Finally, as Father Marc'hadour so movingly put it at the end of our Saturday sessions, More believed not that conscience was some given, unalienable right, but rather that it was the duty of each man to form his own conscience rightly. To quote More's own words: "Any man is bounden, if he see peril, to examine his conscience surely by learning and good counsel and be sure that his conscience be such as it may stand with his salvation." [16] Perhaps conscience, like conciliarism, was something which More had gradually come to achieve.

One might say, in general, that the morning papers (Schoeck and Elton) on each day of our symposium, had concentrated on More as a public figure, viewing him primarily in his roles of lawyer and king's councillor and

15. Rogers, no. 216, p. 557: "[Cromwell] said that I had ere this when I was chancellor examined heretics . . . And he said that I then, as he thought and at the leastwise bishops did use to examine heretics, whether they believed the pope to be head of the church and used to compel them to make a precise answer thereto."

16. Rogers, no. 211, p. 547. See also Marc'hadour's discussion of conscience in *Moreana* 1 (1963): 58.

diplomat. That this subject—More's active life—could by
no means be divorced from his inner meditations was amply
evident in the way in which the themes of silence and
conscience were generated in the ensuing discussions. Our
afternoon papers, on the other hand, stepped back, so to
speak, from More as a public servant in order to study, as
Professor Martz did, a particular period of his literary
career (the Tower works) or to establish, as Father Marc'-
hadour developed his paper, the essential features of his
spirituality during the earlier years of his life. Yet here
too, although the focus was inward, it became clear that
More's private concerns were intimately connected with his
active life in the world. Professor Martz was led to observe
that, if More could accept the right of parliament to
legitimize the children of Anne Boleyn, he nonetheless was
at best ambiguous in his references to "the Queen's Grace"
(Katherine or Anne?).[17] Father Marc'hadour too, in his
treatment of More's attitude toward truth, had occasion to
adduce several of More's "white lies" as he conducted the
complicated negotiations over the payment of Erasmus' pension. Personal integrity was not an issue here, but the ways
of the world, as More himself often noted,[18] can sometimes
force the best-intentioned man to entertain a series of viable
compromises.

It might also be argued, particularly in the case of a
complex personality like More's, that a man's public actions
inevitably affect the caliber and the growth of his inner,
spiritual life. More's Tower works, for example, not only
reflect the quality of his heart and soul as he nerved himself

17. This point led to a lively exchange between Professors Martz and
Elton. For a postscript, see the former's note, below, p. 80.
18. Cf., for example, More's interesting remark to Peter Giles (*Utopia,
CW 4*, 41): "Just as I shall take great pains to have nothing incorrect in
the book, so, if there is doubt about anything, I shall rather tell an
objective falsehood than an intentional lie—for I would rather be
honest than wise."

for his execution; they also define for us, forcefully and poignantly, the process of mind in and through which his admirable serenity ("merriness," he called it) was attained.

The very circumstances under which they were composed, as Professor Martz's discussion of the *Treatise on the Blessed Body* showed, have led to a certain degree of uncertainty regarding the sequence in which he wished them to be arranged. As Martz pointed out, if the *Blessed Body* is viewed as the concluding portion of the *Treatise on the Passion* and not as a separate work,[19] then one can discern a gradual development in More's Tower writings that led, at last, to the achieved Christian conviction which he so fervidly expressed in the Latin *Expositio Passionis* and in the marginal annotations to his *Prayer Book*.

Thus we felt, again and again during our sessions, the constant pressure exerted upon More by both the past (his studies of scripture, the classics, the church fathers, the law) and the present (his official and unofficial duties in civil and royal courts and his patriarchal duties in his broad family circle). But these burdens, so cheerfully assumed by him and so assiduously borne, were always being subjected to a counter, self-generated pressure that steadily emanated from his innermost being. He could not be active without being contemplative, but his meditations in turn became part of the structure of his actions—even, in the end, his last grand act, played out on the scaffold of Tower Hill.

The term "contemplative," as applied to More, itself occasioned some spirited discussion. How close was his acquaintance with contemplative writers of the English

19. Most of the commentators found this original argument quite convincing, although some reservations were offered (Professor O'Kelly) about the exact date (before or after More's imprisonment) at which the *Treatise* was composed. Corroborative evidence drawn from Professor Miller's study of the Valencia manuscript of the *Expositio Passionis* is presented below, pp. 81–82, in a footnote to Martz's paper.

Middle Ages like Richard Rolle or Walter Hilton (Dickens)? One might suggest (Martz) that this traditional piety was more Latin and European than peculiarly English and that More's participation in it was yet another link between him and greater Christendom. Similarly, More's view of Erasmus, so ably described by Professor Thompson, is limited in the letters which are extant by his awareness that Erasmus was never particularly interested in the complexities of British political affairs and policy. Erasmus belonged to the large world of humanism, an area from which More's later career forced him, bit by bit, to withdraw— even if, at his trial, he was to reaffirm his allegiance to its universal ideals.

Equally problematical, with regard to More's own piety, is the matter of his devotion to the ascetic values of medieval monasticism. On this point Father Marc'hadour, basing his analysis mainly on the *Letter to a Monk* of 1520, argued that More aligned himself with the Franciscan spirit and practice and not directly with that of the Carthusians with whom he had lived during his early years (ca. 1501–04). Pressed by Professor O'Kelly for a closer definition of this element in More's spiritual life, Marc'hadour emphasized the "sense of community" characteristic of St. Francis, with its spirit of self-sacrifice, its devotion to the crucifix and, above all, its inner and outer (mendicant) freedom. More was not, as Colet and Latimer may have been, a stoical spirit. His humorous acceptance of life, whether it was manifested in the "black comedy" discerned by Martz in Book II of the *Dialogue of Comfort* or in his bourgeois Londoner's love, noted by Dickens, for a smoking-room story, was not always calculated to endear him to others; [20] but it did express an amplitude of soul, an ability to come

20. One is reminded of Edward Hall's final comment on More's character—"I know not whether to call him a foolish wiseman or a wise foolish man."

to terms with God's creation that may indeed be typical of
the Franciscan spirit at its best.

Towards the close of our sessions on Saturday afternoon,
these broader considerations began gradually to emerge.
Perhaps it was not accidental that allusions to *Utopia,*
hitherto almost a "forbidden book," filtered occasionally
into the comments of various speakers. Father Marc'hadour
noted, in response to an earlier query, that atheism was not
a viable position in Utopia. Anyone who denied God or the
afterlife was, in that country, severely penalized. Such views
were construed, by the Utopians, as a kind of madness, and
we were left to ponder how this situation could be related
to More's own views on religious toleration. A. M. Young's
final comment brought us back to the question of truth and
integrity, a central topic in Marc'hadour's paper. Did More
follow Augustine in emphasizing the historical nature of
truth? For the latter, truth was often to be viewed as a kind
of performance in time. Hence its "situational" aspect, with
all of the various possibilities that such a position could
hold for the student who is interested in seeing More as a
most relevant figure for the modern scene.

As we closed, not very far from Utopia, it became clear
that both the active and the contemplative sides of More's
multivalent personality ought to be comprehended under
some sweeping estimate of his basic philosophic principles.
A "Man for All Seasons" was not easy to grasp; only by
bringing a variety of perspectives to the study of his life
and work could we hope to capture something of his essential nature. Professor Marius, late on Saturday afternoon, presented us with a moving depiction of the "in-
carnational theology" that, in his eyes, formed the well-
spring of More's being. Unlike his polemical opponents—
Tyndale especially—More could never reject the material
world as merely physical. He believed, fundamentally, in
the unity of body and soul. He saw man as a complex

entity in whom, ultimately, body and soul must work together. The spiritual life should be mixed with the public
life. Each drew strength from the other and man's proper
condition was the mingled state, various, multifaceted,
harmonious. The vision was not less than noble. Sir
Thomas More and Saint Thomas More were one and the
same man.

RICHARD J. SCHOECK

Common Law and
Canon Law
in Their Relation to
Thomas More

In 1477 Chief Justice Brian had remarked that, "It is common knowledge that the thought of man should not be tried, for the Devil himself knoweth not the thought of man." [1] We shall later return to the question of one's being triable for thoughts and intentions—so close to the perilously balanced point on which More tried to rest his defense: given More's silence (so his argument ran), everyone had the right to suppose that by his silence More was giving assent to the king's Act of Supremacy. The fact is that the civil law maxim which More quoted, *Qui tacet consentire videtur*—or, as Harpsfield renders it, *he that holdeth his peace seemeth to consent* [2]—cuts more than one way, and much depends upon where one stands in the interpretation.

Our concern is with the interface between canon and common law as we find their conflicts and cross-influences in the career and writings of Thomas More. We look toward, although we cannot yet hope to comprehend, the larger role and importance of law in the England of More. Ultimately, that problem should be related both to the practice of the day and also to such criticisms of contemporary legal institutions and practice as those of St. German and Starkey and to such literary satires as those of Skelton and John Heywood.[3] And so, simply to examine the problem with respect to Thomas More, there are two pivotal matters about which this paper will turn. The first is the affair of Richard Hunne (together with the intimately related Standish-Kidderminster debate), because in its central issue of heresy we have a prime area of conflict, and because it is a case which continues to be discussed throughout the lifetime of More and, indeed, resurfaces again in the 1590s in the controversy of Cosin and Morice. The second is the matter of More's own trial, in ways and for reasons which will I think emerge.

The Legal Career of Sir Thomas More

Although he had been admitted to the bar several years earlier than 1510, had served his inn of court (Lincoln's Inn),[4] and had played a notable role in the 1503 Parliament, Thomas More's first significant public legal office was that of under-sheriff of London, which he held from 1510 until 1518. Considering that his mother's father had been sheriff of London in 1503–04, and that much of his father's considerable legal practice had been in the City, Thomas More's appointment as under-sheriff and his continuing close relations with the City and with City companies are more easily understandable.[5]

Plucknett has commented on the extent to which More would have "ministered mingled law and equity as Under-Sheriff," [6] a point to which one returns in developing the consideration that More had long experience in mingling law and equity before becoming Lord Chancellor. During his under-sheriff years, More seems to have moved into some work with maritime and international law, both of which drew heavily upon the procedures of Roman rather than common law. His most famous case in this field came in about 1517, his defense of the papal right to a ship which

Henry had stopped at Southampton and claimed as a forfeiture. More was retained as counsel and interpreter for the papal interests, and the case was heard in Star Chamber before Wolsey and other judges, where (Roper accounts in his biography),

> Sir Thomas More not only declared to the ambassador the whole effect of all their opinions, but also, in defence of the Pope's side, argued so learnedly himself, that both was the foresaid forfeiture to the Pope restored, and himself among all the hearers, for his upright and commendable demeanor therein, so greatly renowned, that for no entreaty would the king from thenceforth be induced any longer to forbear his service.[7]

This case of the Pope's ship explains why More never became a serjeant, for this event was preceded by his absence of some months on the 1515 embassy to Bruges (during which he was permitted to fill his office of under-sheriff by deputy and during which he wrote the major part of the *Utopia*). Normally, having done his two readings at Lincoln's Inn, he would have soon been made serjeant; and eventually so distinguished a common lawyer would have become a common-law judge. Instead, as we know, More was drawn into the king's service as councillor. A second point. In this case of the Pope's ship, as during the trade negotiations at Bruges, More manifested the results of study and experience in jurisprudential thought with a range and depth which has yet to be probed; clearly he demonstrated skill in the procedures of both Roman and canon law. His admission to Doctors' Commons in 1514 is now more understandable, yet still remarkable, for here is a common lawyer admitted to a professional association of established (if not all distinguished) civilians without a formal period of study at a university with recognized faculties in the two laws, and indeed without any academic

degree—much less the advanced degree in law and the
specialized ecclesiastic or equivalent practice that were
required (at least a little later, if not in 1514).[8] On his
subsequent embassies to Bruges in 1520–21, references were
made in the confidential Hanseatic dispatches to More's
skillful handling of 'multasque rationes, jura, leges et
canones'.[9] And other activities during the 1520's would have
developed still further More's legal expertise in Roman
and canon law—all before he became Chancellor in 1529.

In 1524 he was made high steward of the University of
Oxford, and a year later of the University of Cambridge
as well.[10] These high stewardships were quasi-judicial, for
in addition to other duties More was involved (at one of the
unrulier periods in the history of those universities) in
trying persons accused of crimes, though of course, as
Chambers notes, there were also aspects which More found
pleasant. In 1525 More succeeded Sir Richard Wingfield
as Chancellor of the Duchy of Lancaster, a separate administration of many lands, estates and possessions; here
More's offices were partly administrative, but doubtless
largely judicial. The modern More scholar must disagree
with Chambers' statement that "very little which interests
us today is recorded of the business which came before
him in the Duchy Court," for Margaret Hastings has been
at work on this business for some years and has shown how
potentially rich the extant records are. In a paper given at
the Anglo-American Conference in 1965 she stressed the
freedom of the Chancellor of the Duchy to operate at a
farther remove from "extraneous pressures . . . royal whims
and demands . . . and the larger forces of change in
Europe":

As Chancellor of the Duchy, he was the king's lieutenant
for the administration of justice, but, instead of having to
administer it through king's Council, Star Chamber,

Masters of the Requests, and Chancery, he could perform all his judicial duties within the one court beginning in his time to be regularly called the Court of Duchy Chamber.

She stresses the fact that the procedures of this court were more flexible than those of the Chancery, and that since 1485 More's predecessors had been laymen, generally trained like More himself in one of the Inns of Court.

If there ever had been a clash between common law and equity, there is no obvious evidence of it in the Duchy records. In Marny's time, 1509–1523, and probably also in More's, when important decrees were given, the chief common law justices of the Duchy were present and party to the court's decisions.

Professor Hastings' conclusion is that More "emerges from the details of the cases as a hardworking administrator, a peacemaker more concerned to get at the causes of violence in the countryside than to inflict harsh punishments, a protector of the weak against the strong, and an astute lawyer who could cut through the mass of detail to the heart of the matter in hand."

From the earliest days of his legal practice, More seems to have been known for his skill in arbitration—and it must be declared that Tudor arbitration is a problem that needs much research and evaluation—for More was involved in some of the most complex estate questions of his day, to take but one kind of practice.[11] Both his literary activities, dealt with by Professor Martz, and his inner devotional life, discussed by l'Abbé Marc'hadour, are vital dimensions in the totality of More; but let us never forget that he was continuously a busy man of the law,[12] who spent most of his waking hours in by far the greatest portion of his adult life reading petitions and other legal documents, hearing evidence and questioning witnesses, giving legal opinions or decisions. We can begin to appreciate the force of his lament that the law (to borrow Bacon's later metaphoric phrase) "drinks too much time." Or, as More himself wrote Peter Gilles (another busy humanist-lawyer) in 1516:

> I am constantly engaged in legal business, either pleading or hearing, either giving an award as arbiter or deciding a case as judge. I pay a visit of courtesy to one man and go on business to another. I devote almost the whole day in public to other men's affairs and the remainder to my own. I leave to myself, that is to learning, nothing at all.
>
> When I have returned home, I must talk with my wife, chat with my children, and confer with my servants. All this activity I count as business when it must be done —and it must be unless you want to be a stranger in your own home.[13]

At the age of about fifty-two he was appointed Lord Chancellor of England, and he served from October 1529 to May 1532. He was of course not the first layman chancellor, but he was the first in many years. Even if we bear in mind Maitland's dictum that medieval clerics were not all canonists any more than they were all saints, what is notable is that for some time the chancellor had traditionally been the Archbishop of Canterbury (Morton and Warham) or York (Wolsey). Consequently, he was a cleric trained in and usually educated in canon law, probably Roman as well, and hence a person with a background that equipped him to apply equity in his administration of the formalized common law which lay to his jurisdiction as chancellor.[14] Let us recall, too, that he had a staff of professionals to aid and guide him.

More's own practice had taken him into Star Chamber and Chancery proceedings, and he would long have known that equity was there applied; and how it was applied. In

1528 St. German began to develop his arguments for the greater application of equity in the common law, in the first Latin dialogue of what later became his celebrated *Doctor and Student*—a few years later expanding the ground of his argument to differences in procedure between common and canon law; and by 1533 More would be deep in controversy with St. German over conflicts between the two procedures, notably over the *ex officio* oath in heresy matters, as will shortly be seen in my discussion of the Hunne affair.

Thus, one may pinpoint the moment of crisis when More's predecessor was concluding his long tenure in the office of Lord Chancellor. In 1528 two influential books appeared in England, which in different ways brought to bear upon the common law concepts of canon and/or Roman law: Christopher St. German's *Doctor and Student* and John Perkins' *Profitable Book*—the first published in Latin, the second in Law-French, and both with remarkable printing histories. At about this time a copy of a 1526 *Decretum* of Gratian was bought by the son of a chief justice of Common Pleas and annotated throughout. From these and like clues, it would appear that the study of canon law by common lawyers was more widespread than has hitherto been supposed.[15]

The Case of Richard Hunne

The affair of Richard Hunne occupied Englishmen of all classes for three decades, and the problems of interpreting this complex affair are still of prime concern to historians of Lollardy and the growing Lutheranism in Tudor England, to students of the ecclesiastical courts at the end of the Middle Ages, and to the potential biographer of Thomas More.[16] For historians, indeed, it has been a matter of controversy for the past four centuries.[17] Here, our concern is to locate the events of this affair in the context of conflicts between common and canon law,[18] as they pertain to Thomas More.

Richard Hunne was a freeman and merchant of London, a well-to-do member of the Merchant Tailors, and a citizen widely known (as More testified) [19] for his charitable practices and fair dealing. Overnight his name became a rallying-cry for lay grievances against the clergy, and his legal causes generated a conflict between ecclesiastical and secular jurisdiction that foreshadowed the cutting of the canon-law ties between England and Rome.[20]

The facts of his story are as follows.[21] His baby son, an infant of five weeks, died on March 29, 1511, and the rector of the parish demanded the child's christening robe (or binding-sheet) as a mortuary; the father refused. The rector, Thomas Dryffeld, having waited one year, brought suit against Hunne for the mortuary on April 26, 1512, suing in the archbishop's Court of Audience.[22] Two days later Hunne was summoned and on May 13 appeared before the court, where he denied the truth of Dryffeld's declaration; but Tunstal [23] pronounced judgment on that date in favor of the rector. This much we know. What is not certain is the sequence of all the ensuing court actions, or details of the pleadings in them. It is clear that on December 27, 1512, Hunne was addressed by the parish priest with these words: "Hunne thowe arte accursed and thowe stondist accursed"; and that the priest refused to proceed with vespers until Hunne left the church. On January 25, 1513, Hunne instituted a suit for slander against the priest, and in Hilary term his suit for praemunire was filed.[24] Apparently Hunne had been accused of heresy by this time, but he was not summoned until December 1514; a commentary on the sequence of events and on the individual suits with the reasoning for this dating will be given below. On December 2, 1514, he was finally brought before the bishop of London on charges of heresy, and two days later (before any action was taken by the bishop) he was found hanged in his cell in the Lollards' Tower; a coroner's jury was impanelled, but did not return its verdict until February 1515.[25] Meanwhile, on December 10 a Paul's Cross sermon was preached against Hunne; on the sixteenth he was signified *post mortem;* and his corpse was turned over to the secular arm and burned at Smithfield on December 20, 1514. The child had died in March 1511, and Hunne himself in December 1514: the turbulent case had taken three years in the courts, and everyone was discussing it.

Against this background, and that of Leo X's 1514 bull pronouncing that laymen had no jurisdiction over churchmen in certain matters,[26] Parliament met in February 1515, with a sermon by the Abbot of Winchcombe at the opening of Convocation that was immediately the focus of public attention and itself the basis of yet another cause célèbre. For Kidderminster preached against Parliament's renewal of an act of 1512 (4 Henry VIII, c.2), known as the Criminous Clerks Act, by denying any distinction between major and lesser orders. All orders were holy orders, he insisted, and therefore any clerk was immune from the punishment of lay tribunals for criminal offenses; this was an open challenging of the accepted practice of the common law, and it was presented as doctrinal and with intransigeance.

D. S. Chambers and M. J. Kelly have argued that "little by little the laity were encroaching, serpent-like, upon ecclesiastical dominion," and the bull *Supernae dispositionis* "contained the massive consolation of several clauses dealing hard blows upon the laity." [27] Clerical morale must have been strengthened by this bull, and "there is every likelihood that the renewed confidence aroused by the Lateran Council's decree lay behind the notorious case of

Richard Hunne . . . . Certainly the decree inspired some strong opinions to be voiced." The Lords, where the spiritualty held the majority vote, dropped the statute that would have renewed the act of 1512, although commons had passed a bill to renew it. At this point Dr. Henry Standish, then warden of the Franciscan friars in London (later rewarded with a bishopric), defended the 1512 act and argued that the decree of Leo X had never been received in England.

On April 17, 1515, the court of aldermen of London appointed a committee to speak with the bishop of London about the matter, for in February the coroner's report on Hunne's death had been shown to the jury and the jury found that Hunne had been murdered by the jailor and his assistant, together with the bishop of London's chancellor, Dr. Horsey. Feelings of London citizens ran high indeed. Small wonder that the historian Polydore Vergil should have recorded on March 3, 1515, that a great outcry arose in England,[28] and still less wonder that the popular mind should have linked the particular issue of Horsey as the accused murderer of Hunne with the more theoretical issue of criminous clerks and the debate of Standish and Kidderminster. The two issues are certainly intimately connected in the legal memorandum incorporated in Keilwey's Reports.[29] It is not too much to say that the debate that joined these issues established not only a collision course between elements of the common and canon law in England, but also a direct challenge to canon law jurisdiction; yet here, as elsewhere, old socio-religious institutions survive within a new frame of reference.

The 1515 Convocation sermon of Kidderminster was the focus of the resentments of members of Commons and of others, and the speaker of the house was part of a group that requested the king to have the issues argued further.

Accordingly, the king chose lawyers and theologians to argue the points involved before various judges and theological counsel at Blackfriars on March 10, 1515.[30]

There Dr. Henry Standish defended the act of 1512 and asserted that a papal decree which forbade the conventing of criminous clerks before a temporal judge as *peccatum in se* had never been received in England. To the Commons' request that the abbot renounce his opinions publicly at Paul's Cross, the bishops replied that they would maintain those opinions with the utmost power. Parliament (and convocation) were prorogued from April 5 till November, but during this recess Standish continued to defend his position in public lectures. And Dr. Horsey was still in custody,[31] while Standish was at large. But in November Standish was summoned before convocation and presented with four questions:

(1) can a secular court convent clergy before it?
(2) are minor orders holy or not?
(3) does a constitution ordained by pope and clergy bind a country whose use is to the contrary?
(4) can a temporal ruler restrain a bishop?

The thrust of these questions is all too obvious, and the importance of Standish in the eyes of contemporary ecclesiastics can be judged by the note of one who was in 1515 both clerk of the parliaments and prolocutor of convocation. In the record of both assemblies, he wrote: "in this parliament and convocation there arose the most dangerous discords between the clergy and the secular power over the liberties of the church; and the minister and the fomenter of all the trouble was a certain friar-minor of the name of Standish." [32]

Against the questions or charges put to him in convocation, Standish appealed to the king for protection. The reply of the bishops was that they were proceeding against Standish not for his counsel to the king (as he was one of

the king's spiritual counsel) but for his public lectures elsewhere. Both the Commons and the bishops exhorted the
king's aid in accordance with his coronation oath, the first
to maintain his temporal authority to the full and the
second to leave Standish to the judgment of the church.

A second meeting of judges, the king's counsel, and
some of the Commons, took place at Blackfriars to consider
Standish's answers to the charges of convocation. One
question discussed was the 'reception' of papal decrees
and the dependence of their validity in England upon
reception there. The judges of the common law eventually
declared that those clergy who were present at Standish's
citation were guilty of *praemunire*. With the vague but
terrible threat of *praemunire* over their heads,[33] the bishops
felt themselves teetering on the edge of the temporal
sword. It would seem that the way of compromise had been
worked out before the next meeting took place at Baynard's
Castle, a royal palace by the river, adjoining Blackfriars.

At Baynard's, Wolsey (as Hughes so aptly remarks) [34] "began his career as a cardinal as he was to end it, kneeling before the king and begging his mercy from the pains and penalties of praemunire"; but there is more of a pattern even
than this to Wolsey's career, for in 1529 he would be compelled to admit that he had tried to subject England to a
foreign-based canon law. (It must be observed that the very
term "canon law" changes in the period from 1515 to 1535;
but this demands further study.) Before a great assembly of
both houses of parliament, of the common law judges, and
of all the king's council, Wolsey knelt before Henry and
made a partial submission and a partial defence. The clergy
for whom he was spokesman had no desire to diminish the
royal prerogative, he said, but they did feel that the matter
of bringing clerics before lay judges was contrary to the
laws of God and an infringement of the liberties of the

church. Wolsey thereupon begged the king to allow the matter to be determined by the pope and his counsel at Rome. Henry's reply was that Standish had already answered all points; in an ensuing general discussion Foxe and Warham supported Wolsey, and the chief justice of the king's bench, Fineux,[35] observed that the clergy could not determine questions of murder or felony and asked what point there could be in committing clergy to courts where they could not be tried. Henry finally ended the discussion by declaring that he would maintain the rights of his crown and temporal jurisdiction as fully as his progenitors had done; as for the bishops, he observed, they had always been able to find a way round canonical obligations whenever it suited them. When Warham put forth the plea to delay the decision until the clergy could place the matter before the pope for a solution (at the cost of the clergy), Henry apparently remained silent, thus withholding his consent.[36]

Convocation proceeded no further with its charge of heresy against Standish, and a royal investigation of the murder charge against Horsey found no real case against him—the attorney general accepted his plea of "not guilty" and the case went no further. But Dr. Horsey had to pay an enormously heavy fine (estimated at £8000 four decades ago) [37] and he lost out in his ecclesiastical career, having to turn to preferments outside of London.[38] Standish, by contrast, was made a bishop: the name of the place, St. Asaph, being satirically turned by some into "Seynt Asse".[39]

Compromise had indeed been achieved, but only a thin, a perilously thin, covering had been placed over the real issues and problems. The heavy hand of Wolsey kept the lid on until 1529, but by that time Lutheranism had come to England and the lid would stay on no longer. Tyndale and St. German, a cleric and a layman, a theologian and a common lawyer, led the campaign for reform, and both made charges about the Hunne affair which Thomas More answered in his writings from 1529 to 1533.[40]

Some further commentary is needed on the Hunne case. The rector's demanding a child's christening robe as a mortuary payment was customary,[41] though it was a legal right often open to abuse.[42] It may be that Hunne's argument in refusing lay in denying that the robe belonged to the baby, but this argument would surely have been put forward in earlier, and unsuccessful, tests of mortuary payments. Disputes in London, as C. H. Williams [43] noted, had occurred as recently as 1501 and 1502, and there is no reason to believe that the citizen there involved did not purge himself as he was ordered to do. One aspect of the case not previously discussed is the fact that the child died in the parish where he had been put to nurse, the father belonging to another parish, and that Dryffeld was the rector of the parish where the child died, not the parish where the father lived: [44] this may well have been a new ground of Hunne's refusal to pay a mortuary to Dryffeld, and may explain why Dryffeld waited a year to bring suit against Hunne at Lambeth. In any event, Hunne did appear before Tunstal, who was then not chancellor of the diocese but chancellor of Archbishop Warham and auditor of causes; a distinguished canonist, he was already a member of Doctors' Commons and later Master of the Rolls.[45] The issue was found for Dryffeld by Tunstal, but there is no indication that Hunne paid or intended to pay; however, excommunication was normally indicated as consequent upon a failure or refusal to pay.[46] It is strange, then, to learn that although this case was over by May 1512, Hunne was apparently not accursed by the parish priest before December 27, 1512—well beyond the traditional forty days.[47]

The usual assumption here is that the parish priest's denunciation (in December 1512) followed merely upon Hunne's failure to make the mortuary payment as he had been ordered by the bishop in the preceding May. It is possible, but not I think likely, that Hunne had begun process for a suit of praemunire before December (and that this would have been the cause of his denunciation); but we cannot be sure. We know only that the praemunire is recorded in Hilary term, 1513, and is preceded by an action against the same Henry Marshall for slander, which was sued out on January 25, 1513.

Thomas More thought that Hunne "was detected of heresy before the premunire sued or thought upon," as he wrote in the *Supplication of Soules*.[48] In that case, the parish priest's denunciation in December 1512 would have been for heresy, not for refusal to pay a mortuary. This explanation would clarify the sequence, but if the denunciation were for heresy, the long delay before his being summoned becomes an element that needs explanation; it may well be that the heresy process was simply set aside until the praemunire issue was settled. The inference from the available evidence is that Hunne's demurrer in the praemunire suit had been argued in the Michaelmas term of 1512 and effectively decided against him, and that a formal judgment would have been entered in Hilary term 1513, but that he was by that time dead.[49]

In the winter of 1512–13, the scope and power of praemunire had not yet been fully determined, but the penalties were severe: complete loss of lands and goods, at least.[50] In his praemunire suit, Hunne named Dryffeld as the principal defendant, but joined with him as *abbettatores, excitatores, procuratores, fautores & consilarii* were his proctor (Gotson), his doctor advocate (Stone), the witnesses (four), the parish priest (Marshall), and the summoner (Charles Joseph, who would later be suspected of

Hunne's murder.) The defendants' plea was that the whole process was lawful. To this Hunne demurred: *minus sufficiens est in lege.*[51]

Two possible pleas were open to Hunne—that mortuaries as property ought not to fall within the jurisdiction of a spiritual court, or that the whole ecclesiastical system was a foreign system of law—but we do not know if he made use of either, the proceedings having been lost. More tells us that the decision would certainly have gone against Hunne:

> it appeared clearly to the temporal judges and all that were any thing learned in the temporal law, that his suit of the praemunire was nothing worth in the king's law, for asmuch as by plain statute the matter was out of question, that the plea to be holden upon mortuaries, belong unto the spiritual court.[52]

The inference to be drawn from More's comment is that the jurisdiction of the spiritual court was clearly recognized by all, and that no one had challenged that jurisdiction, at least, not recently. However, the statute or writ *Circumspecte Agatis* (13 Ed. 1, 1285), while it limited ecclesiastical courts to what was then interpreted as strictly ecclesiastical business, could be seen as carrying royal assent to that business.[53]

Hunne was denounced by the parish priest on December 27, 1512, and claiming damage to reputation and business he instituted suit for slander. It is no doubt significant that in the rolls this immediately precedes his praemunire action; it is remarkable that his fellow-merchants seem to have reacted already (in response to some ecclesiastical pressure), and one must ask whether Hunne was in fact *vitandus* by the end of 1513. To this bill for slander, Milsom comments, the defendant demurred; "and again the record ends with a series of adjournments, the last being to the term after Hunne's death." And while there are earlier examples of slander in the common-law rolls—and slander itself is an action that later crosses from ecclesiastical to secular jurisdiction—"I have not seen one trenching so obviously as this on the ecclesiastical jurisdiction," and it would indeed be very instructive to have a report of argument on a demurrer in so early a case.[54]

While much has been made of More's friendship with Tunstal, not enough stress has been put on More's close connections with the city and its companies, which at that time would have biased him toward London merchants rather than the hierarchy; for in addition to his quasi-judicial office as one of the two under-sheriffs of London from 1510 to 1518, he acted for or with a number of the London companies on legal and business matters (being very intimately involved with the Merchant Adventurers), and from 1510 to 1512 he represented the City in Parliament.[55] But there is one further connection, seldom noted: More was brother-in-law of the lawyer-printer John Rastell, who was later given wardship of Hunne's two daughters.[56]

While at first reading More does not seem concerned with questions of the conflict of jurisdiction in the Hunne case, we must consider the context of the oft-cited chapter in the *Dialogue:* first, that it belongs to the year 1528–29, a period of vigorous anti-clericalism, short of an outright split with Rome; and second, that it is part of a literary dialogue, and in this chapter More is dealing only with what the Messenger knows by hearsay about the Hunne affair. Consequently More chooses to discuss the case only in this light—and his treatment is rather humorous, both to discredit the rumors and to induce the reader to see the case in a chosen perspective. Shortly afterward, the case again appears in a controversial work, *The Supplication of Souls,* in which More is answering similar charges made

in Simon Fish's *Supplication of Beggars,* a violently anti-
clerical work. (A year or two later, the common lawyer
Christopher St. German will attack More from another
quarter, but that must be a later chapter in this complex
story.) For now, we must simply declare that in the *Dialogue* and the *Supplication* More is answering allegations
and rumors about the handling of the heresy charges
against Richard Hunne—no more. However, we do learn
that bitterness about the case continues in London nearly
twenty years later, and we can test More's essential accuracy
in his handling of facts, even though he does not present
the full story.

It would seem to be nearly impossible to determine from
this distance whether Hunne was murdered or was a
suicide. The facts are these: that he was found hanging in
his cell after being examined before the bishop on a charge
of heresy and while still in the custody of the bishop; that
the clergy imputed his death to suicide, held a trial *post
mortem* for heresy, and condemned and released his body
to the secular arm for burning; that shortly thereafter a
coroner's jury found that he had been murdered and returned a verdict against the bishop's chancellor, Dr. Horsey,
and others; but the attorney general, when the case was
brought to arraignment before the Court of King's Bench
(after, it must be noted, the resolution of the Standish-
Kidderminster debate) allowed a plea of 'not guilty' and
the case was permitted to be dropped. (A *nolle prosequi,*
we would say today.) All of this is expounded in several
places in More's writings, and he tells us in his *Dialogue*
that he knew the case intimately:

> So well I know it from top to toe that I suppose there be
> not very many men that knoweth it much better. For I
> have not only been divers times present myself at certain
> examinations thereof, but have also divers and many

times sunderly talked with almost all such, except the
dead man himself, as most knew of the matter.[57]

I do not know how to explain the contradiction with a
passage written five years later which very strongly implies
that More *had* talked with Hunne:

> And yet for because I perceived in him a great vain-
> glorious liking of him self, and a great spice of the same
> spirit of pride that I perceived before in Richard Hunne
> when I talked with him . . . .[58]

If the phrase "when I talked with him" is to refer only to
Thomas Philipps and not to Hunne, then this is a very care-
less sentence on a crucial point.

More thought, from his knowledge of the case, that Horsey was not guilty. He was also convinced that Hunne had
been a heretic, and in the *Dialogue* he brings forward
the evidence of an Essex carpenter accused of heresy
six or seven years after Hunne's hanging, who named
Richard Hunne as one of those who came together secretly
for heretical readings.[59] But the strongest argument by
More is that,

> Myself was present in Paul's when the bishop, in the
> presence of the mayor and the aldermen of the city,
> condemned him for an heretic after his death. And then
> were there read openly the depositions by which it was
> well proved that he was convict as well of divers other
> heresies, as of misbelief toward the holy sacrament of
> the altar. And thereupon was the judgment given that
> his body should be burned, and so was it. Now this is
> quod I to me a full proof.[60]

When we turn from the Hunne affair to that of Standish,
the evidence is less contradictory; the issues are clearly
drawn, and perhaps the clearest is the opposition of Stan-

dish and Kidderminster, the direct challenging by Kidderminster of the common law position and the direct challenging by Standish of the traditional liberties of the
church.[61] Further, it is clear that the king consulted carefully with his theological counsellors on the progress of the
Standish matter and that his decision was final and, for
the future of church-state relations in England, absolutely
determinative.[62]

Thus the king's assertions of his view of sovereignty and
jurisdiction is to be studied with care:

> By the ordinance and sufferance of God we are King of
> England, and the Kings of England in time past have
> never had any superior but God alone. Wherefore know
> you well that we will maintain the right of our Crown
> and of our temporal jurisdiction, as well in this point
> as in all others, in as ample a wise as any of our progeni-
> tors have done before us. And as to your decrees, we are
> well informed that you yourselves of the Spiritualty do
> expressly contrary to the words of many of them, as has
> been well shown to you by some of our spiritual Coun-
> sel; nevertheless, you interpret your decrees at your
> pleasure. Wherefore, consent to your desire more than
> our progenitors have done in time past we will not.[63]

The influence of this affair upon More's career and
thought deserves some attention. First, it is difficult to believe that it would not have colored his thinking during
the months he was away from England immediately after
the meeting of Parliament in February 1515 and while he
was writing the first draft of his *Utopia* during his Flemish
embassy. This collision of the spiritual and the temporal
laws, together with the failure of the Fifth Lateran Council
to achieve reform, surely go far (as I think) to explain the
note of urgency in Book I of the *Utopia*.[64] And while there
is little in More's writings that is a direct commentary on

the criminous clerks question, it is worth recalling that in
his *Utopia* those priests who commit any offence whatsoever suffered no temporal punishment; instead, they were
left only to God and their own consciences:

> . . . even if they have committed any crime, they are
> subjected to no tribunal but left only to God and to
> themselves. They judge it wrong to lay human hands
> upon one, however guilty, who has been consecrated
> to God in a singular manner as a holy offering. It is
> easier for them to observe this custom because their
> priests are very few and very carefully chosen.[65]

Further, in view of the king's words that in effect closed
off discussion of the jurisdiction of the temporal and spiritual, it is not necessary to credit More with the gift of
prophecy to explain some of the anecdotes foreshadowing
his own position in 1530 which his biographers recount.

The above passages from Thomas More's writings dealing with the Hunne affair have been torn from their contexts in very different works, and something must therefore
be said about their weight and usefulness. One must here
also stress the obvious: More's cited writings are all in the
vernacular, whereas heretofore (except for satirical references like those in Skelton or in Fish's *Supplication*) discussion of the canon law would have been in Latin. Christopher St. German's writings are notable for pioneering
the discussion of equity, procedure and other matters in
English. Inevitably there would be problems of termi-
nology (for example, in citations and in translating Latin
tags familiar enough to those trained in canon law); but
other less obvious difficulties emerged as well. This I must
defer for later treatment.

At no time did More sit down to write out a full brief
on the Hunne affair. In his *Supplication of Souls* he is
answering Simon Fish's satiric and often deliberately ex-

aggerated attack in *A Supplication for the Beggars* (1528);
in his *Dialogue* (1529), he is dealing with the Lutheran
case, but the mood, the control, the pace, are such that one
can read with good humor—and in Book III, chapter 15,
More's fullest treatment of the Hunne affair, he persuades
the Messenger that the popular notions are misconceptions.
The remaining works which refer to Hunne are in one respect at least of a kind. The *Confutation,* the *Apology,* and
the *Debellation* are answers (the first to Tyndale, the
second and third to Christopher St. German, though he
wrote anonymously and More did not identify his anony-
mous opponent with the author of *Doctor and Student*)—
they have a common method, and a common tone which
is anything but good-humored.

The greater part of the *Debellation* is devoted to More's
defense of the existing laws for the investigation, and trial,
and punishment of heretics. In his conclusion,[66] he almost
misses St. German's main thrust. For More lays the consent
of the general council and "the general approbation of all
christian realms" against the changes which St. German
proposes: but that is precisely what St. German denies,
for he is doing nothing less than challenging the traditional
system of canon law, with its authority, procedures and
jurisdiction. More argues: "against this general approbation he layeth his own reason. And what is his own irre-
fragable reason?" The Hunne case is therefore presented
with a greater urgency by St. German. To Fish, it had been
an example of what results from a court system whose procedure is secret; but he scarcely challenges that system as a
whole. St. German is challenging the system, and he uses
the Hunne affair as an example; his division of spirituality
and temporality (given that it was conventional enough) is
deliberately a dividing, with a lessening and subordinating
of the spirituality. (But a detailed study of the debate be-

tween More and St. German on canon vs. common law must be a matter for further study.)

C. S. Lewis has aptly characterized More's case against the heretics as being in his books as the soul is in the body; *"tota in toto et tota in qualibet parte;* that the reader, whatever page he lights upon, should find there all that he needs for refutation of the enemy." [67] While the individual points made by More are clear enough, and these have been brought forward *seriatim* in discussing the several aspects of the case, we must bear in mind that we do not have More's full view of the affair—as we do have that of, for example, Hall; [68] that the tone changes with each work; that there are differing degrees of modification; that even the dialogue form must be read differently. [69] *Caveat lector* must be writ large for all historians who turn to literary works for evidence, though there is much to be gained from such enterprises.

As to More's view of the conflict between common law and canon law that emerges during the Hunne affair and the sequential Standish case, at this stage of More studies I can only assert my opinion that More did not accept the dominant view of Commons (perhaps, though not certainly, that of a majority of English common lawyers) that Parliament could solve disputed points of canon law. Rather, as Derrett has pointed out, [70] he shared the continental view that Parliament could not. But much further study of More's legal writings and of his legal philosophy needs to be done. [71]

To generalize from only this one example would be to act like the tourist who exclaimed, "all Indians walk in single-file. At least the one I saw did." Yet this one case, with its wealth of secondary materials, points clearly toward a wider body of events, evidence and literature, and toward several conclusions. First, no one can deny that

there was current a general dissatisfaction with the ma-
chinery of the courts Christian; "popular feeling, in London
at any rate," a distinguished Tudor historian has written,
"had been inflamed by quarrels between the laity and the
ecclesiastical courts over church-dues and jurisdiction",[72]
and there was much bitterness toward the secrecy of the
ecclesiastical courts.[73] The dry wood needed only a strong
spark to burst into flame. The coroner's jury and its find-
ings, together with the popular outcry over Hunne's death
and against Dr. Horsey, point to what our generation can
call only a credibility gap. And there seems to be very little
evidence that the Fifth Lateran Council, then sitting, was
sufficiently concerned with these matters which so deeply
troubled the laity; clearly, there was no effort to commu-
nicate what efforts had been made toward reform to the
laity.[74] It was in England that the effulgent figure of Wolsey, as Pollard graphically writes, "had been invoked to
pale the ineffectual fires of an insurgent house of commons
and to quench the flying sparks of schism in the church":
fires of insurgency there were, and everywhere a great cry
for reform, but revolt and schism came only after these
fore-warnings had been continuously ignored by Rome.[75]
This early in the history of the Reformation, it is notable
that Richard Hunne was a merchant; not that heresy or
even strong anti-clericalism was a characteristic peculiar
to his class, but that Hunne as a merchant enjoyed a high
degree of independence, and a high social status, whereas
the city's parish clergy tended to be of a much lower social
position.[76] This much we can say with firmness: when the
stand was taken against what so many of the London
citizenry had long considered the unreasonable demands
of the clergy, particularly in areas of mortuary and ecclesiastical procedure, it is no surprise that such a stand was
made by a merchant of independent mind and means.[77]

What is now needed is a close study of other individual

cases, for the argument of statistics may overlook the depth of the issues or the heat of the feelings involved, as has often been the case, in my view, with the Hunne affair. To turn to a recent study, that of F. Donald Logan, which so admirably charts normal procedures and outlines the development of excommunication and the use of the secular arm:

> For the period up to the Reformation about 7,600 significations of excommunication survive, of which about 2,800—roughly one-third of the total—date from the thirteenth century. These records are without parallel in Western Europe, just as, it would appear, the English procedure against excommunicates as a highly formalized and institutionalized procedure was itself without parallel. What they reveal is a practical area in which close cooperation—not wholly without irritants—characterized the relations of the ecclesiastical and secular jurisdictions.[78]

Cooperation there was and long had been in England between secular and ecclesiastical jurisdictions, but it turned on a perilous balance. While one would not use so anachronistic a concept as the consent of the governed here, nonetheless it would appear that in England the close cooperation of which Logan speaks was possible, and would continue, only so long as the secular power so consented. Once challenged seriously, and with the tacit support of the king, the force of the ecclesiastical arm fell to the ground. Further, it follows, if my reading of the Hunne case is accurate, that the Reformation in England began in 1515 but was interrupted. Checked by a number of forces—not least by the enormous and then-increasing concentration of power in the hands of Wolsey (much of it illegal, i.e., contrary to or without the sanction of existing canon law)—the Reformation was suppressed until 1529. Then, at the time of Wolsey's fall (though not primarily for that

reason), the forces for reform began to swell, and there is
merit in echoing the cliché that the 1529 Parliament, the
so-called Reform Parliament, began where the 1515 and
1523 Parliaments had left off. These observations and conclusions have an important bearing on the history of the
Reformation in England; but for the moment, I would
urge that the Hunne affair is vital for understanding the
relations between ecclesiastical and secular jurisdictions
in England: and that, from a reading of the case as has
here been put forward, one would have to conclude (for
England at least) that the long-overdue reform of the canon
law (which had been on the agenda of the Fifth Lateran
Council) was in fact too late to prevent the gathering
storm, even if it had been successfully dealt with before
the close of that council in April 1517. For the split had
been widening in 1515, and by October 1517 it was already
too late.

The Trial of Sir Thomas More

Before such an audience as this, there is no need to re-
capitulate the story of More's trial—already well told by
Chambers, it has more recently been twice told by Reynolds, and there is of course the version by Bolt in *A Man
for All Seasons,* which has already influenced the way that
our students picture and think of the trial. Yet some aspects deserve commentary in the light of our present discussion.

Long imprisoned in the Tower: yet the length of that
imprisonment, while it grabs our hearts with fear and pity,
the length is not so extraordinary as the quality of the
solitary life More lived there, as we know from the evidence of the *Prayer Book* and from the Tower writings
that Professor Martz will discuss. The final events in More's
case moved swiftly, after the trial of John Fisher on June 17,

1535, and his beheading on June 22. A grand jury at Westminster returned a true bill against More, described as 'late of Chelsea', on June 28, and the trial was set for July 1. Crucial to the concluding part of the indictment is the charge of the jurors that "the aforesaid Thomas More, falsely, traitorously, and maliciously" deprived the king of the dignity, title, and name of the Supreme Head on earth of the Church of England.

More's first reply stressed the fact that he was being tried under acts passed while he was imprisoned, and that during this time of imprisonment he had kept silent on all matters pertaining to the State.

> Touching, I say, this challenge and accusation, I answer that, for this my taciturnity and silence, neither your law nor any law in the world is able justly and rightly to punish me, unless you may besides lay to my charge either some word or some fact in deed.[79]

It is at this point that More argued that

> if the rule and Maxim of the civil law be good, allowable and sufficient, that *Qui tacet, consentire videtur* (he that holdeth his peace seemeth to consent), this my silence implieth and importeth rather a ratification and confirmation than any condemnation of your statute.[80]

More, it is clear, rested his case upon this subtle principle, supported as it was by civil law tradition—but he was speaking to men trained in the common law, not civilians or even canonists. It was a delicate principle, and the tactics of arguing upon it to such a body of judges must be seen as a desperate remedy. I love the man this side of idolatry and heresy—but sometimes it is heuristic to look for the other side of the story or argument—for historians, biographers, or lawyers. So I shall for a moment play the *advocatus diaboli*.

Professor Elton has recently reminded us of how relatively undeveloped the law of treason was on the eve of the
Henrician Reformation, and so it was. Mere treasonable
utterances had already been construed by fifteenth-century
common-law judges as constituting an overt deed within
the meaning of the statute of 25 Edw. III, st.5,c.2 (1352):
words, it is clear, "were quite often treated as equivalent to
overt deeds in trials of treason." [81] There may be an analogy between St. German's *some say* and More's *put case,*
the one for heresy, the other for treason.

It is then, perhaps not so remarkable that the woolier
minds among the Tudor common lawyers could with some
force of sincerity have believed that the withholding of
consent, particularly by the king's former lord chancellor,
be construed as treasonable. Greatness or high place gave
no security against the suspicion of treason, as we know
from the histories of the Buckinghams, Poles, Wyatts, and
others during the reign of Henry VIII.

Then there is the quite different matter of Rich's testimony. It does More no good now, as it would have done
him no good then, to point out that generally in ecclesiastical matters involving good faith, contracts, and the like,
two witnesses would have been required; certainly, in heresy proceedings, it would be most unusual to find fewer
than two witnesses to establish the guilt of the accused.
Heresy was a kind of treason of the soul: there are parallels, and we should not be surprised by an awareness of
such parallels. But on this point, at least, the courts christian would have given a witness somewhat more safeguards
than did the court that tried More.

Roper quotes two of More's speeches in some detail, and
they are so vital that they must be quoted again here.
While speaking to the discharge of his own conscience and
to the demurrer that the particular law under which he

was being charged was contrary to the laws and statutes of England, he cites Magna Charta:

> Quod Anglicana ecclesia libera sit, et habeat omnia iura sua integra et libertates suas illaesas.[82]

As he was speaking thus against the intrusion of the authority of the state into a field reserved, as he argued, to the church, More was interrupted by the chancellor, Audley, who asked More if he set his judgment against that of so many learned men, the bishops and the universities.

> To that Sir Thomas More replied, saying: "If the number of Bishops and universities be so material as your lordship seemeth to take it, then see I little cause, my lord, why that thing in my conscience should make any change. For I nothing doubt but that, though not in this realm, yet in Christendom about, of these well learned Bishops and virtuous men that are yet alive, they be not the fewer part that be of my mind therein. But if I should speak of those which already be dead, of whom many be now holy saints in heaven, I am very sure it is the far greater part of them that, all the while [they] lived, thought in this case that way that I think now. And therefore am I not bound, my lord, to conform my conscience to the Council of one Realm against the general Council of Christendom."

The thrust of More's conciliar thought surfaces here: his argument and appeal are anchored upon a General Council of Christendom, not upon a pope, and least of all upon the single historic figure who was then sitting in the chair of Peter. Although it may be said that this is a theological, or ecclesiological point, I would insist that it does have very deep implications for More's legal thought. His notion of the universal competence and jurisdiction of the canon

law of the church of Christendom is involved, and he
would not subordinate that law to the law of one realm.

One final point, and as Roper contains the entire matter
within a single paragraph, I shall read him entire:

> Now when Sir Thomas More, for the avoiding of the
> indictment, had taken as many exceptions as he thought
> meet, and [many] more reasons than I can now remem-
> ber alleged, The Lord Chancellor, loath to have the
> burden of that judgment wholly to depend upon him-
> self, there openly asked the advice of the Lord Fitz
> James, then Lord Chief Justice of the Kings Bench, and
> joyned in commission with him, whether this indict-
> ment were sufficient or not. Who, like a wise man, an-
> swered: "My lords all, by St. Julian" (that was ever his
> oath), "I must needs confess that if the act of parlia-
> ment be not unlawful, then is not the Indictment in my
> conscience insufficient."

It was indeed, to echo Reynolds on this point, rather late
in the day to question the sufficiency of the indictment, and
Fitzjames's answer is most guarded: if the Act of Parliament was lawful, then the indictment is sufficient. But if it
were not? Fitzjames's guarded reply (couched in the nega-
tive), does not dare to go that far. Yet that, surely, is the
point.

That Thomas More lived in a complex age is a truism.
Indeed, one might well quip that all ages are complex (to
those that live in them), only some are more complex than
others. Yet Tudor historians and all scholars dealing with
the literature, thought, and institutions of the period
would substantially agree that there were profound trans-
formations taking place within the lifetime of Thomas
More, and not least within the legal institutions, the concepts, and the very language of the law. But More himself
did not question—ever, anywhere, so far as I know—the

organic notion of the two arms of the law, the secular (or civil) and the ecclesiastical. He was responsible only for the first of these (as lord chancellor); the second (as a layman) he did not control, yet in it he played a significant, if as yet undetermined role.

It seems unmistakably clear to me that More was a legal amphibian, who could move and did work within the two systems and within their interface—and, still further, that he believed in the possibility, indeed the necessity, of the two systems working together. If a dissenter were to ask, didn't everyone? I should have to answer quite firmly, no. There were many who fought the power or the abuses of the ecclesiastical system, men like Roy and Tyndale and a number of others—and perhaps those who complained against the language, or power, or mysticism of the common law provide a needed parallel—but certainly there was at least one who wrote powerfully and persuasively against the ecclesiastical system *in toto:* Christopher St. German. Thomas More was not writing against straw men; there was a challenge, and from 1529 to 1534 he tried to meet that challenge. After 1532, May 15 to be precise, with the Submission of Clergy, he must have known that he had failed, that the fight was lost. Why then continue the fight? There was first the effort to defend the church or the hierarchy, or even more importantly what More conceived as the faith of Christendom, against charges which he thought inaccurate or unjust, and progressively malicious. There was secondly the hope of changing the minds, or modifying the views, of the many who would otherwise be won straight over by advocates of the New Lutheran Learning. But I think as much as anything there was that in More which could not abide a false case or position and have it win by default: simply, he had to answer St. German.

To a lawyer like More, the matter of jurisdiction which

was so much the heart of the Hunne affair was a vital matter, and it connected intimately with his own case. After the verdict had been delivered in his own trial, and only then, More gave forth his mind in one last great speech, as we all know, declaring that he had all the councils of Christendom and not just the council of one realm (and councils of the past, not just the minds of the present) to support him in the decision of his conscience. If the Hunne affair turned upon the jurisdiction of two courts over a mortuary garment and the attendant causes between a layman and his parish priest, his bishop, and so on, More's trial turned on the Erastian question of state dominion or jurisdiction over the church and his conscience. More died, not so much for any one historic pope —friend of Erasmus and of so many diplomats with Roman experience that he was, he could have had no illusions about Julius or Leo, or Clement VII, their dilatory successor who helped the Reformation to come to a boil in England through his calculated strategy of doing nothing over Henry's divorce proceedings—or even for an isolated general notion of the papacy. More's death resulted directly from his belief that no lay ruler could have jurisdiction over the church of Christ, and his concept of the church was more compatible with a post-Vatican II concept than with a Tridentine one.

Born into a lawyer's family, trained in the household of an ecclesiastic who was both Archbishop of Canterbury and Lord Chancellor of England, schooled in the common law to which he devoted so much of his mature life and skilled in much of the lore and technique of the civil and canon laws as well, More died as he had lived: a lawyer who accepted and practiced within a double legal system that until the eve of the Reformation had functioned, with its delicate balances, as an implicitly organic structure of two arms of the law. If they did not always reinforce or complement each other, at least they had managed to co-exist—less than perfectly, of course, but with considerable efficiency and no little justice—and he could not accept the subordination of one system to the other.

NOTES

1. Year Book 17 Edw. IV. Pash. 2, quoted by Lord Reid in his lecture on "The Law and the Reasonable Man," *Proceedings of the British Academy* 54 for 1968 (1970): 198. "Comen erudition est qui l'entent d'un home ne ser trie, car le Diable n'ad conusance de l'entent de l'home," in Law-French. Thomas Brian, or Bryan, studied in Gray's Inn and was named chief justice of the common pleas in 1471. He apparently served until his death in 1500. He was the grandfather of Francis Bryan, the friend of Sir Thomas Wyatt and himself a scholar and poet.

2. Harpsfield's *Life of More,* ed. E. V. Hitchcock (London, 1932), p. 186. This Roman maxim is imbedded in the canon law: see "De Regulis Iuris" of Bonifacius VIII in *Sexti Decretal.,* Lib. V., Tit. xii (Richter-Friedberg, *Corpus Iuris Canonici* [1959 rpt.], 2: 1123). For a modern discussion, see Thomas H. Davis and Carl Landauer in the American Historical Association *Newsletter* 8 (September, 1970): 15 and 9 (January, 1971), 21–22.

3. See my "Satire of Wolsey in Heywood's Play of Love," *Notes & Queries* 196 (17 March, 1951): 112–14, and "Canon Law in England on the Eve of the Reformation," *Mediaeval Studies* 25 (1963): 125–47.

4. See my "Thomas More & Lincoln's Inn Revels," *Philological Quarterly* 29 (1950): 426–30.

5. Chambers, pp. 171, 192.

6. T. F. T. Plucknett, *A Concise History of the Common Law* (London, 1956), p. 697.

7. Roper, pp. 9–10; cf. Chambers, p. 152.

8. See my "Canon Law in England," p. 142.

9. Ibid.

10. Chambers, pp. 214–15.

11. A number of arbitrations recorded in the London City Records, dating from 1510 to 1517, and again in 1524, are given in the historical notes to Harpsfield's *Life of More,* pp. 312–14. The arbitration in 4 Henry VIII (1513) of the estate of Catherine, Countess of Devonshire, involved Archbishop Warham, John Fineux (then Chief Justice of the Court of Common Pleas), together with Richard Elyot and Lewis Pollard, both king's serjeants, and Thomas More. Cf. *Statutes of the Realm* (1817), 3; 57, and the comment of A. F. Pollard

in *Historical Essays in Honour of James Tait* (London, 1933), p. 236, *n. 2*.

12. See my "Thomas More, Humanist and Lawyer," *University of Toronto Quarterly* 34 (1964): 1–14.

13. *Utopia, CW 4,* 19–41.

14. See "More, Humanist and Lawyer," and "Canon Law in England."

15. St. German was educated in the Middle Temple and Perkins in the Inner Temple. More's inn of course was Lincoln's Inn, which had been Fortescue's (in whose writings canon law concepts frequently occur). It is clear that professional interest in the canon law was not limited to a single inn, but one cannot say whether it was taught at all, or whether this interest depended altogether upon the individual lawyer. Worth exploring too is the new factor of the growing number of men who had begun, if not completed, their education at Oxford or Cambridge, where they might have encountered some canon and Roman law before going down to the inns.

16. This portion of my essay is drawn from a paper given at the Fourth Congress of Medieval Canon Law in Strasbourg, 1968. There is no convenient bibliography of the Hunne affair, but there are the following modern discussions: E. Jeffries Davies, in *Victoria History of London*, 1: 236 f., and "The Authorities for the Case of Richard Hunne (1514–15)," *English Historical Review* 30 (1915): 477–88. Kenneth Pickthorn, *Early Tudor Government—Henry VIII* (Cambridge, 1934, rev. ed., 1951), pp. 112–14; A. F. Pollard, *Wolsey—Church and State in Sixteenth-Century England* (New York, 1966), pp. 32 f.; Arthur Ogle, *The Tragedy of the Lollards' Tower* (Oxford, 1949); Philip Hughes, *The Reformation in England*: 1, 'The King's Proceedings' (London, 1952): 149 f.; S. F. C. Milsom, "Richard Hunne's 'Praemunire'," *EHR* 76 (1961): 80–82; J. Fines, "The Post-Mortem Condemnation for Heresy of Richard Hunne," *EHR* 78 (1963): 528–31.

17. Since the writing of More and Foxe in the sixteenth century; for early historical discussions of the Hunne affair, see Davies, "The Authorities," pp. 477 f.

18. Conflicts there were, despite continuing statements to the contrary; the matter has been put most tersely by F. W. Maitland: "about certain matters a quarrel with the See of Rome was maintained from century to century" (*Constitutional History of England* [Cambridge, 1908], p. 507). Yet the history of that conflict has not yet been written.

19. More writes that Hunne "trusted to be spoken of long after his days and have his matter in the years and terms called Hunne's case" (*Dialogue Concerning Heresies,* Book III, ch. 15, ed. W. E. Campbell et al. [London, 1927], p. 239), but the case is not even noted in many histories of the English law. More acknowledges that Hunne was "as they that well know him say he was indeed . . . a fair dealer

among his neighbours" (*Dialogue*, p. 239); and Polydore Vergil wrote of Hunne as "as especial father of the poor, for it was ever his way to give help to the needy" (in *Anglicae Historiae* [1555 ed.], p. 645; quoted by Ogle, *Lollards' Tower*, pp. 48–49).

20. See my "Canon Law in England," pp. 131–32.

21. The facts are stated in the pleadings of his *praemunire* action in the King's Bench roll for Hilary term, 4 Henry VIII (1513): see S. F. C. Milsom in *EHR* 76, pp. 80 f.

22. Dryffeld sent Henry Marshall, his chaplain and parish priest at Whitechapel, to start suit for the recovery of the bearing-sheet at Lambeth (Milsom, p. 80).

23. It has been traditional to describe Tunstal as a friend of More, but we do not know when their friendship began. See note 45 below.

24. In his slander suit, Hunne complains that he went to hear vespers, and Marshall, "ready in his surplice to say them,

ex sua malicia precogitate . . . excelsa voce dixit ista obprobiosa & minatoria verba ad procuracionem litis et ad dampnum tam corporis quam bone fame ipsius Ricardi Hunne . . . Hunne thowe arte accursed and thowe stondist acursed and therfore go thowe oute of the churche for as long as thowe arte in this churche I wyll sey no evynsong nor servyce *ubi in facto predictus Ricardus Hunne non est nec adtunc fuit excommunicatus . . .*

whereupon Hunne *ad evitandum magis malum & ob metum lesionis corporis sui* left the church *et vesperas ejusdem diei & festi . . . totaliter amisit;* and his good name and credit were so damaged that the merchants with whom he ordinarily dealt dared not and would not trade with him" (Milsom, pp. 81–82).

25. See Ogle, *Lollards' Tower*, pp. 81–82.

26. *Bulla reformationis curiae*, May 1514, in *Conciliorum Oecumenicorum Decreta*, pp. 597–601.

27. In an unpublished essay on the English bishops and the 5th Lateran Council.

28. Thus Polydore Vergil, writing to Rome from London on March 3, 1515: see Pollard, *Wolsey*, p. 39 and *n.*

29. *Relationes quorundam Casuum selectorum ex libris Roberti Keilwey . . .* (S.T.C. 14901); with other editions, 1633, 1688. On the authorship of these reports, see A. W. B. Simpson, "Keilwey's Reports, Temp. Henry VII and Henry VIII," *Law Quarterly Review* 73 (1957): 89–105.

30. For the account of events which follows, I am indebted to Pollard's narrative in *Wolsey*, pp. 45 f.

31. In the charge of Archbishop Warham.

32. Quoted by Pollard, *Wolsey*, p. 51.

33. Praemunire (also spelled *primunire*) figures in the Year Books, but the extent of its use with respect to ecclesiastical jurisdiction was

still to be defined. But behind praemunire (stat. 16 Rich. II, c. 5) lay
the statute or writ of *circumspecte agatis*, which operated in its fairly
well-defined area of action. Of this writ, Maitland has written:

> Both parties were in turn aggressors. In 1373 the commons in
> parliament complain that the courts Christian are encroaching to
> themselves pleas of debt even where there has been no lesion of
> faith, and it seems plain that the ecclesiastical judges did not care
> to inquire whether a complainant could have found remedy in a
> lay court. On the other hand, the king's justices would concede
> but a small territory to the canonists; their doctrine is that the
> only promises that are subject for spiritual jurisdiction are promises
> which concern spiritual matters. (P&M, 11, 201)

Cf. W. S. Holdsworth, *History of English Law* (London, 1923–64) 1:
586; W. T. Waugh, "The Great Statute of Praemunire," *EHR* 37
(1922): 173–205; and E. B. Graves, "The Legal Significance of the
Statute of Praemunire," *Anniversary Essays . . . Charles Homer Has-
kins* (Boston and New York, 1929), pp. 57–80. More himself warned
the king of praemunire (see note 53 below).

34. *Reformation,* 1: 153.

35. Another connection with More: Fineux's daughter and heiress,
Jane, was married to John Roper, whose son William was More's
'son Roper' (married to Margaret More in 1521) and his biographer.
See E. M. G. Routh, *Sir Thomas More and His Friends* (London,
1934), p. 131.

36. Perhaps in 1535 Henry would recall this one case where silence
did not mean consent.

37. Pollard, *Wolsey,* p. 51n.

38. Ibid., p. 51; see also Ogle, *Lollards' Tower,* p. 159. Some of the
preferments which Horsey held before 1511 he continued to hold until
as late as 1543 (see John Le Neve, *Fasti Ecclesiae Anglicanae,* 1: 104;
5: 18, 38, 64; 7: 8; 8: 73; 9: 62). But his office of archdeacon of London
was terminated in 1514 (5: 9).

39. Hughes, *Reformation,* 1: 154 and n.

40. From the time of his license to read Lutheran books in 1528,
he wrote the following: *Dialogue Concerning Heresies* (1528), *Supplication of Souls* (1529)—he became Chancellor in October 1529 and
resigned May 16, 1532—*Confutation* (I, 1532; II, 1533), and *Apology,
Debellation and Answer To The Book . . .* (all 1533).

41. See M. M. Sheehan, *The Will in Medieval England* (Toronto,
1963), p. 300, on local customs, and notes 328 ff. on authorities cited.

42. On the mortuary payment as customary in England, see
W. Lyndwood, *Provinciale* (1679 ed.), pp. 21–22, and Christopher St.
German, *Treatise . . . Spirituality & Temporalty,* ch. 9. On gar-
ments as mortuaries, see Powicke & Cheney, *Councils and Synods*
(Oxford, 1964), 2: pt. 2, 1050 n. 4. Revision of mortuaries would come

only in stat. 21 Henry VIII, cap. 6; they were still a matter of controversy in St. German's *Salem and Bizance* and More's *Debellation*
(1533).

43. *England under the Early Tudors* (1925), pp. 196–97.

44. The infant died in the parish of St. Mary's (Whitechapel),
where it had been put to nurse; Thomas Dryffeld was the rector of
this parish. Richard Hunne lived in the parish of St. Margaret's,
Bridge Street, close to London Bridge. See Ogle, *Lollards' Tower*,
p. 51.

45. See A. B. Emden, *Biographical Register of University of Oxford*
(Oxford, 1957–59), 3: 1914.

46. Powicke and Cheney, *Councils and Synods*, 2: 1051–52. See
further Lyndwood, *Provinciale*, s. *Mortuarium*.

47. In England, as Logan has noted, a period of 'more than forty
days' (*quadraginta dies et amplius*) was sufficient to establish obduracy
after the imposing of excommunication: F. D. Logan, *Excommunication and the Secular Arm in Medieval England* (Toronto, 1968), pp.
72–73.

48. *EW*, p. 297: "Now is it of truth well known, that he was
detected of heresy before the premunire sued or thought upon. And
he began that suit to help to stop the other withal, as indeed it did
for the while. . . ."

49. Milsom, p. 81.

50. See notes 16 and 42 above.

51. Milsom, pp. 80–81. "The defendant who demurs admits the
facts, but contends that the facts give the plaintiff no cause for action.
A Demurrer therefore raises an issue of law" (Holdsworth, *HEL* 3:
474 *n.*).

52. *Supplication, EW*, p. 298.

53. See note 33 above. Thus, there is an irony in More's own warn-
ing to the king of the statute of Praemunire, "whereby a good part of
the Pope's pastoral cure here was pared away" (Roper, pp. 67–68).
Cf. Chambers, p. 194.

54. Milsom, p. 82.

55. On More and the City, see Chambers, p. 171 and 103, and note
11 above. For an illuminating view of the City's right to legislate,
see J. Duncan M. Derrett, "Thomas More and the Legislation of the
Corporation of London," *The Guildhall Miscellany* 2 (1963): 175–80.

56. A. W. Reed, *Early Tudor Drama* (London, 1926), pp. 9–10.

57. *Dialogue (EW,* p. 235).

58. *Apology* (1533), ed. A. I. Taft (London, 1930), p. 142.

59. Cf. Ogle, *Lollards' Tower*, pp. 102–03.

60. *Dialogue (EW,* p. 239).

61. "It has an interest for the historian," Knowles has commented,
"as being the last occasion when a monk and a friar stood forward
as recognized spokesmen on a living issue of religious policy and

theory, and it is noteworthy that each filled his historical role: the monk as the high churchman defending privilege, the friar as the advocate of the anti-clerical, anti-papal party" (D. Knowles, *Religious Orders in England* [Cambridge, 1961], 3: 54).

62. "Not even Wolsey could, or tried to, govern in defiance of the king or without consulting his wishes, a point which might be illustrated at length from such major issues as the cases of Richard Hunne and Friar Standish down to little details" (G. R. Elton, *The Tudor Revolution in Government* [Cambridge, 1953], p. 66).

63. Keilwey, quoted by Ogle, *Lollards' Tower*, p. 153. Translated from the Law-French of the original.

64. See my brief discussion in the *New Catholic Encyclopedia*.

65. *Utopia, CW 4*, 229. It seems to have escaped notice and discussion, in this context, that an earlier piece of Tudor legislation enabled the punishing of priests and other religious men for dishonest living (stat. 1 Hen. VII, c.4, 1485), and that stat. 4 Hen. VII, c.13, 1489 was an act to take away the benefit of clergy from certain persons.

66. *EW*, p. 1031.

67. *English Literature in the Sixteenth Century* (Oxford, 1954), p. 174.

68. Edward Hall in *English Historical Documents,* ed. C. H. Williams (London, 1967), 5: 660–64.

69. Cf. Lewis, pp. 172–74, for a close look at this vital consideration.

70. "The Trial of Sir Thomas More," *EHR 79* (1964): 470. We know that More debated parliament's legislative capacity with German civilians in 1520: see *Hanserecesse 3* (ed. D. Schafer, 1905), 7: 583–611 (Derrett *loc. cit.*).

71. I have endeavored to say more on this in my forthcoming Yale lectures, *Thomas More and the Law*. See "Canon Law in England," esp. 136 and *n.*, and also "Jean Bodin and the Opposition to Thomas More and the Mixed State," to appear in the *Proceedings of the Jean Bodin Seminar* (1971).

72. Thus Pollard, *Wolsey*, p. 31; cf. 38 n. 3. Pollard viewed the Hunne affair as part of "a protest against ecclesiastical jurisdiction by a middle-class laity clamouring, for the first time, for self-determination" (p. 27).

73. There is much in Tyndale that voices that bitterness against the secrecy of the procedure in courts of canon law, especially in his *Obedience* (see Hughes, *Reformation*, 1: 136–37). An extreme (and somewhat inaccurate) statement has recently been made that "one of the causes of the overthrow of the Roman church in the sixteenth century was the layman's hatred of the petty tyranny of the ecclesiastical courts—tyranny which produced in 1515 the scandal of the death of Richard Hunne in the Bishop of London's prison": Alan Harding, *A Social History of English Law* (London, 1966), p. 255. But one of

the key documents, certainly, in the English Reformation is Parliament's Supplication against the Ordinaries, which in 1532 complained against procedures in the spiritual courts (see Pickthorn, *Henry VIII*, pp. 180 f.). In the same year St. German, who continued his attack upon spiritual courts in a number of anonymously printed pamphlets, reprobated "the making of laws by the church, which they had none authority to make" (*Spiritualty and Temporalty*, ch. 12; see Pickthorn, p. 165, n.3, and F. L. Baumer, *Early Tudor Theory of Kingship* [New Haven, 1940], pp. 66 f.).

74. On the general cry for reform there is a vast literature; for a convenient recent summary statement, see John W. O'Malley, 'Historical Thought and the Reform Crisis of the Early Sixteenth Century,' *Theological Studies* 28.3 (1967), with its excellent focus on Giles of Viterbo, whose famous sermon at the opening of the 5th Lateran Council so admirably captures the need and sentiment for reform.

75. *Wolsey*, p. 58. From Rome's point of view, no doubt, the established order was running well enough. "The sheer weight of custom resisted all demands for the internal reform of the Church," as Knowles has written, and things went on without too much being questioned; the Church in England "continued to pursue its old paths, an unchangeable and apparently impregnable institution, mechanical no doubt in its processes, restrained from beneficial innovations by the prevailing spirit of legalism . . . the smooth and placid immobility of the ecclesiastical system."

76. In Sylvia Thrupp's *The Merchant Class of Medieval London* (London, 1948), pp. 180–88, there is much on the merchant as parishioner, and some evidence for his high degree of independence. But recent studies of Lollardy (by A. G. Dickens and others) have shown that the merchant was a key figure in the history of the Reformation.

77. Thrupp has found no "evidence of disapproval of the monastic order" among merchants, but at the same time "no instance has come to notice of any London merchant being so overcome by religious emotion as to give up his way of conducting life and enter a religious order" (ibid., p. 188).

78. Logan, p. 24.

79. Harpsfield, p. 185.

80. Ibid., pp. 185–86.

81. G. R. Elton, "The Law of Treason in the Early Reformation," *The Historical Journal* 11 (1968): 211–36, especially 232 and n.

82. Roper, p. 93.

LOUIS L. MARTZ

Thomas More:
The Tower Works

In the traditional view, we may apply the phrase "Tower Works" to those writings of More which are contained in the last 320 pages of Rastell's great folio of 1557—those works which the editor specifically identifies with the statement: "made in the year of our Lord 1534 by Sir Thomas More Knight, while he was prisoner in the Tower of London," or words to that effect. These are, in the order of their folio printing: "A Dialogue of Comfort"; "A Treatise to Receive the Blessed Body of our Lord, Sacramentally and Virtually Both" (a very short work, less than six pages); "A Treatise upon the Passion of Christ (unfinished)"—in Rastell's title; "to which," says the editor, More "made this title following," which I quote in part: "A treatise historical, containing the bitter Passion of our Savior Christ, after the course and order of the four Evangelists, with an exposition upon their words . . . beginning at the first assembly of the bishops, the priests, and the seniors of the people, about the contriving of Christ's death. . . . And it endeth in the committing of his blessed body into his sepulchre . . ."[1] This last is the English treatise on the Passion, which of course breaks off long before the scene at the sepulchre; it ends with More's long exposition of the meaning of the sacrament established at the Last Supper.

And as it breaks off, in the midst of "The third lecture of the sacrament," the editor notes: "Sir Thomas More wrote no more in English of this treatise of the Passion of Christ. But he (still prisoner in the Tower of London) wrote more thereof in Latin (after the same order as he wrote thereof in English), the translation whereof here followeth." [2] Then follows Mary Bassett's translation of her grandfather's Latin treatise, of which the holograph manuscript was discovered in Valencia in 1963—More's own rough draft, with many revisions.[3]

But at this point one must cast doubt upon the validity of some of the editor's statements concerning the Tower Works in the edition of 1557. (I shall call the editor "Rastell"—though we cannot be sure that he made all the editorial remarks and titles.) As we note in Miss Rogers' edition of More's *Selected Letters*, Garry Haupt has found a letter from More to his secretary, John Harris, written from Willesden (now in northwest London, but then of course a separate village outside of London). In this letter More asks Harris to correct a certain learned matter concerning the paschal feast which occurs about half-way through the English treatise on the Passion. "I put you in remembrance of this," says More to Harris, "because I have mistaken it in the paper that you have." [4] The paper in Harris's possession, one would assume, must be a draft of More's treatise on the Passion, of which Harris was perhaps making a fair copy. Clearly then, some part, if not all, of this English treatise had been written before More entered the Tower; and one might wish to speculate that it was the intervention of More's imprisonment that caused the breaking off of the English treatise and the change to Latin for its sequel. Since the two are in such close sequence, Rastell could well have assumed that they were written under the same conditions—especially since More might have taken the English treatise, or a part of it, into the Tower with him, intending to complete it there. However this may be, Rastell is highly circumstantial concerning the Latin treatise which follows. In a prefatory note he says that More began the Latin treatise, "being then prisoner, and could not achieve and finish the same, as he that ere he could go through therewith (even when he came to the exposition of these words, *Et iniecerunt manus in Iesum*) was bereaved and put from his books, pen, ink, and paper, and kept more straitly than before, and soon after also was put to death himself." (Note how the word *himself* stresses the parallel between Jesus and More.) [5]

Finally, we have the miscellany gathered together by Rastell at the close of the great folio: "Certain devout and virtuous instructions, meditations, and prayers made and collected" by More, and best of all, the great series of last letters written from the Tower.[6]

I say, best of all, because they constitute our best account of More's conduct during his interrogations and imprisonment, our best account of his state of mind, and, it is not perhaps too much to say, some of his finest works of art. These final letters are works of *art,* in every sense of that word, for they show the most artful regard for the presence of two or three or more different audiences. More could have no doubt that every letter he wrote might be carefully read by his keepers, perhaps even sent to Cromwell himself, who was, as More well knew, alert to every phrase which might entrap More into a confession or a recantation. One has the sense that when, for example, More is writing his account of his interrogation at Lambeth,[7] he is interested not only in sending a clear account of what happened to his daughter Margaret and thus to all his family. He is also taking the occasion to clarify and stake out his position to anyone who might happen to read the letter; meanwhile, he engages in some sharp plays of wit. "In that time saw I Master Doctor Latimer come into the garden, and there walked he with divers other doctors and chaplains of my Lord of Canterbury, and very merry I saw

him, for he laughed, and took one or twain about the neck
so handsomely, that if they had been women, I would have
went [i.e., thought] he had been waxen wanton." Or note
the apparent touch of irony in his account of how he was
temporarily dumbfounded by Cranmer's argument that,
in doubtful matters, one is bound to obey the king: "yet
this argument seemed me suddenly so subtle and namely
with such authority coming out of so noble a prelate's
mouth, that I could again answer nothing thereto but only
that I thought myself I might not well do so, because that
in my conscience this was one of the cases in which I was
bounden that I should not obey my prince." Or consider
the incongruously gentle compliments that More so cere-
moniously pays, while recording the rough oath of Cromwell: "Upon this Master Secretary (as he that tenderly
favoreth me), said and sware a great oath that he had
lever that his own only son (which is of truth a goodly
young gentleman, and shall I trust come to much worship)
had lost his head than that I should thus have refused the
oath." [8]

Later on, in a long letter which a servant has secretly
carried to Dr. Wilson,[9] his fellow-prisoner in the Tower,
one feels that More's verbosity is a way of conveying the
fact that he is really unwilling to say anything to Wilson
about the problem that they both face. In one place in
particular I think we can detect more than a little mark of
More's slyness, as he writes to Wilson concerning "divers
faults found in the bull of the dispensation, by which the
King's Council learned in the spiritual law reckoned the
bull vicious, partly for untrue suggestion, partly by reason
of unsufficient suggestion."

Now concerning those points I never meddled. For I
neither understand the doctors of the law nor well can
turn their books. And many things have there since in

this great matter grown in question wherein I neither
am sufficiently learned in the law nor full informed
of the fact and therefore I am not he that either mur-
mur or grudge, make assertions, hold opinions or keep
dispicions [i.e., disputations] in the matter, but like the
King's true, poor, humble subject daily pray for the
preservation of his Grace, and the Queen's Grace and
their noble issue and of all the realm, without harm
doing or intending, I thank our Lord, unto any man
living.[10]

More's naive ignorance of these doctors of the law may well
arouse a smile; and what shall we make of his concluding
assertion that he prays daily "for the preservation of his
Grace, and the Queen's Grace and their noble issue"?
Which queen? Which issue? We know that there was in
More's eyes only one true queen, and it was not Anne
Boleyn.[11]

Most artful of all is that marvellous letter allegedly
written by Margaret Roper to Alice Alington,[12] giving
an account of the conversation with her father, by way of
answer to Alice's letter relating the two fables she has been
told by Audley.[13] Rastell's comment on this artful piece
of writing gives us the right clue: "But whether this answer
were written by Sir Thomas More in his daughter Roper's
name, or by herself it is not certainly known." [14] The
arguments of More in this letter are so circumstantially
given, and the language has such a resonance of his own
style, that I think one ends up with very little doubt that
this letter is primarily More's own composition. One can
imagine More and Margaret planning it together and
speaking much of it aloud in More's Tower room. But
its art seems to me all More's.

This letter is a prime example of More's art of improvisation, his art of exploration, an art that seems informal,

extemporaneous, spontaneous. It is an art that allows for long digressions, excursions, and familiar asides, but in the end it reveals, lying under and within all its apparent wandering, a firm and central line, a teleological structure, based on a goal never forgotten. The chief goal of this letter is a defense of what people call More's "scruple of conscience," as described in the opening lines: "if he stand still in this scruple of his conscience (as it is at the leastwise called by many that are his friends and wise) all his friends that seem most able to do him good either shall finally forsake him, or peradventure not be able indeed to do him any good at all." [15] *Conscience* is the key term, more than forty times repeated. The drama of the letter is set in terms of a temptation scene, with daughter Margaret in the role of "Mistress Eve": "hath my daughter Alington played the serpent with you, and with a letter set you a work to come tempt your father again, and for the favor that you bear him, labor to make him swear against his conscience, and so send him to the devil?" [16] But More is thoroughly prepared to meet the temptation, for, as he says: "I have, ere I came here, not left unbethought nor unconsidered, the very worst and the uttermost that can by possibility fall. And albeit that I know mine own frailty full well and the natural faintness of mine own heart, yet if I had not trusted that God should give me strength rather to endure all things, than offend him by swearing ungodly against mine own conscience, you may be very sure I would not have come here." [17] After three pages carefully setting up the situation, we then find Margaret giving More her sister's letter to read: "Thereupon he read over your letter. And when he came to the end, he began it afresh and read it over again. And in the reading he made no manner haste, but advised it leisurely and pointed every word." [18]

Here we find More presenting himself in the very process

of creating one of his artful improvisations. One has the impression that More never speaks or writes spontaneously, or extemporaneously. He speaks and writes only after the line and goal of his work have been firmly established. So now he explodes Audley's first fable, by showing that this was one of Cardinal Wolsey's favorite tales, and what the results of following it were: "But yet this fable, for his part, did in his days help the king and the realm to spend many a fair penny." [19] As for Audley's second fable, that of the lion, wolf, and ass, More finds "surely it is somewhat too subtle for me." But he manages somehow to deduce that he is the foolish ass in the eyes of Audley, and of many others, too.[20] Then, after the merry tale of the man named "Cumpany," More's voice rises to a solemn tone as he reaches at last the goal of his discourse, declaring for his daughter's comfort the stalwart firmness of his conviction:

> But as concerning mine own self, for thy comfort shall I say, daughter, to thee, that mine own conscience in this matter (I damn none other man's) is such as may well stand with mine own salvation. Thereof am I, Megge, so sure, as that is, God is in heaven. And therefore as for all the remnant, goods, lands, and life both (if the chance should so fortune), sith this conscience is sure for me, I verily trust in God, he shall rather strength me to bear the loss, than against this conscience to swear and put my soul in peril, sith all the causes that I perceive move other men to the contrary, seem not such unto me as in my conscience make any change.[21]

Then he rounds out the dramatic framework by returning to the image of a temptation, saying: "How now, daughter Marget? What how, mother Eve? Where is your mind now? Sit not musing with some serpent in your breast, upon some new persuasion, to offer father Adam

the apple yet once again." [22] And so the letter concludes
with the temptation firmly overcome and with Thomas
More displaying, to the comfort of his friends and family,
his cheerful, resolute, and loving spirit:

> And with this, my good child, I pray you heartily, be
> you and all your sisters, and my sons too, comfortable
> and serviceable to your good mother my wife. And of
> your good husbands' minds I have no manner doubt.
> Commend me to them all, and to my good daughter
> Alington, and to all my other friends, sisters, nieces,
> nephews, and allies, and unto all our servants, man,
> woman, and child, and all my good neighbors and our
> acquaintance abroad. And I right heartily pray both
> you and them, to serve God and be merry and rejoice in
> him.[23]

And may we add that perhaps More, with his long view of
history and of the Christian community, past, present and
future, had us in mind too, as a part of his possible
audience?

Especially interesting to us, in this context of the Tower
Works, is the very close relation that this letter bears to
the literary method and to the contents of More's *Dialogue
of Comfort*. For this letter is in itself a dialogue of comfort,
and the dialogue between daughter and father bears much
the same tone and manner that we find in the dialogue between those two fictional Hungarians, old Uncle Antony
and young Nephew (or "Cousin") Vincent, as the Great
Turk threatens to overwhelm Hungary with his persecu-
tions. The general subject of this dialogue-letter and the
Dialogue of Comfort is basically the same: how should
the Christian behave when persecutors test his strength
to endure for what he believes, in his conscience, to be the
true faith? A particular analogy between the two dialogues
may be found in More's elaborate fable of the fox, wolf,

and ass, and their scruples of conscience, as told at length
in the *Dialogue of Comfort*.[24] This, it seems almost certain,
is a direct result of More's reading a similar fable in Alice
Alington's letter, and then trying wittily to explicate it
for the benefit of Margaret, himself, and any other readers.
This particular collocation of dialogue technique and subject matter lends very strong support to Rastell's statement
that the *Dialogue of Comfort* was a Tower Work, as indeed
its whole tenor would lead us to believe. But the parallels
between this great letter and the *Dialogue of Comfort* form
only one strand of the many affiliations that tie together
the Tower Works into the one central work that is the
ultimate achievement of all these varied writings: the
preparation of More's mind to meet his death, if God so
wishes.

A rich insight into the nature and manner of that preparation may be gained from considering the sequence in
which Rastell has presented some of these Tower Works,
beginning with the *Dialogue of Comfort* and ending with
the last words of the Latin work on the Passion: *tum de-
mum primum manus iniectas in Iesum:* "then after all
this, did they first lay hands upon Jesus." Only one slight
alteration in the sequence needs to be made, as I shall
explain a little later.

The *Dialogue of Comfort* begins with those two Hungarians discussing the rumors that the Great Turk and his
army are before long likely to overrun that Christian land.
But the possibility is still somewhat remote, in the stage of
rumor and worry, not quite a reality as yet. Appropriately,
the dialogue in Book I of the treatise is rather abstract and
theoretical, dealing mainly in moral platitudes, and indeed
not working at a very high level of concern or interest. But
after the break in time, Book II at once begins with a
stronger current of immediacy, with humorous and worldly
anecdotes, related in a chatty fashion. Then longer and

stronger anecdotes begin to come in, such as the biting and
hilarious fable of the fox, ass, and wolf, which is then
followed by a violent example of black comedy, in the tale
of the carpenter whose shrewish wife tempted him into
chopping off her head:

> As her husband (the man was a carpenter) stood hewing
> with his chip-axe upon a piece of timber, she began after
> her old guise so to revile him that the man waxed wroth
> at last and bode her get her in, or he would lay the helm
> of his axe about her back, and said also that it were little
> sin even with that axe-head to chop off that unhappy
> head of hers that carried such an ungracious tongue
> therein. At that word the devil took his time and whet-
> ted her tongue against her teeth, and when it was well
> sharped, she sware to him in very fierce anger, "By the
> mass, whoreson husband, I would thou wouldest; here
> lieth mine head, lo." And therewith down she laid her
> head upon the same timber log. "If thou smite it not
> off, I beshrew thine whoreson's heart." With that, like-
> wise as the devil stood at her elbow, so stood (as I heard
> say) his good angel at his, and gave him ghostly courage,
> and bode him be bold and do it. And so the good man
> up with his chip-axe and at a chop chopped off her head
> indeed. There were standing other folk by, which had a
> good sport to hear her chide, but little they looked for
> this chance till it was done ere they could let it. They
> said they heard her tongue babble in her head and call
> "Whoreson, whoreson" twice, after that the head was
> from the body. At the leastwise, afterward unto the king
> thus they reported all, except only one, and that was a
> woman; and she said that she heard it not.[25]

The *Dialogue* begins to bulge and almost explode with
this invasion of worldliness; but already, a few pages before
the beast-fable, More has introduced the means by which

this unruly element will be brought under firm control: that great central text from Psalm 90, *Scuto circumdabit te veritas eius*, which dominates the remainder of the treatise.[26]

Finally, in Book III, as the word arrives that "the great Turk prepareth a marvelous mighty army," [27] the immediacy of the threat leads to the composition of what amounts to a treatise on the necessity of meditation: meditation on Hell and Heaven, but most powerfully, most dramatically, meditation on the Passion of Christ, and especially on the Agony in the Garden: "And though you would fain flee from the painful death and be loath to come thereto, yet may the meditation of His great grievous agony move you, and Himself shall, if you so desire Him, not fail to work with you therein." And again, near the close of the *Dialogue:* "In our fear let us remember Christ's painful agony, that Himself would for our comfort suffer before His Passion, to the intent that no fear should make us despair; and ever call for His help, such as Himself list to send us." [28]

After such exhortations More's English treatise on the Passion might seem to form a natural sequel. But what about the intervening brief treatise entitled by More, so Rastell tells us, "To receive the blessed body of our Lord, sacramentally and virtually both"? [29] I would like to suggest another position for this brief treatise; I think that it really is the concluding portion of the incomplete "third lecture" with which the English treatise on the Passion breaks off in Rastell's printing. This "third lecture" is introduced with the declaration, "I have in the first lecture (good readers) expowned you the words of our Savior at the institution of the blessed sacrament. And after have I in the second, showed you somewhat of the sacramental signs, and of the sacramental things, that are either contained therein, or signified thereby." And then he adds, "Now is it convenient

that we somewhat speak, in what manner wise we ought to
use ourself in the receiving. We must understand that of
this holy sacrament, there are three manner of receiving. For
some folk receive it only sacramentally, and some only
spiritually, and some receive it both." [30] Clearly this third
lecture is planned as a short treatise on how to receive the
sacrament. More then describes for two columns in the
great folio the state of those who receive the sacrament
only sacramentally, that is, those who receive it "unworthily."

> But because they receive it in deadly sin, that is to wit,
> either in will to commit deadly sin again, or impenitent
> of that they have committed before, therefore they re-
> ceive it not spiritually: that is to say, they receive not the
> spiritual thing of the sacrament, which as I before have
> showed, is the sacramental thing that is signified thereby,
> that is to wit, the society of holy saints, that is to say, he
> is not by the spirit of God unid [united] with holy saints
> as a lively member of Christ's mystical body. [31]

Then, in a short paragraph that ends the English treatise
as here printed, More explains the second manner of receiving:

> Some, as I said before, receive this blessed sacrament
> only spiritually, and not sacramentally, and so do all they
> receive it which are in clean life, and are at their high
> mass devoutly. For there the curate offereth it for him
> and them too. And although that only himself receive it
> sacramentally, that is to wit, the very body and blood
> under the sacramental signs, the forms of bread and wine,
> yet as many of them as are present at it, and are in clean
> life, receive it spiritually: that is to wit, the fruitful thing
> of the sacrament, that is to say, they receive grace, by
> which they be by the spirit of Christ more firmly knit and

unid quick lively members in the spiritual society of
saints.[32]

Is it possible that More would thus leave the treatise
without the essential third way of receiving, that is, sacramentally and spiritually both? Now consider the opening of
the brief treatise on receiving the sacrament: "They receive
the blessed body of our Lord both sacramentally and virtually, which in due manner and worthily, receive the blessed
sacrament." And then he goes on to warn against taking the
sacrament when we are "unworthy":

> In remembrance and memorial whereof, He disdaineth
> not to take for worthy such men, as willfully make not
> themself unworthy, to receive the self same blessed body
> into their bodies, to the inestimable wealth of their souls.
> And yet of His high sovereign patience, He refuseth not
> to enter bodily into the vile bodies of those, whose filthy
> minds refuse to receive Him graciously into their souls.
> But then do such folk receive Him only sacramentally,
> and not virtually: that is to wit, they receive His very
> blessed body into theirs, under the sacramental sign, but
> they receive not the thing of the sacrament, that is to wit,
> the virtue and the effect thereof, that is to say, the grace,
> by which they should be lively members incorporate in
> Christ's holy mystical body: but instead of that live grace,
> they receive their judgment, and their damnation.[33]

The echo of certain phrases and concepts in the earlier
passage that I have read from the beginning of the third lecture, I think, can leave little doubt that this opening of the
"Treatise to Receive the Blessed Body" is firmly welded to
the third lecture. And this effect is reinforced by the way in
which, on the next page of the treatise on the blessed body,
More repeats in his characteristic way an allusion to St.
Paul's statement in the first epistle to the Corinthians, con-

cerning those who "eat the bread and drink the cup of our
Lord unworthily." [34]

Why, then, does More use here the word "virtually,"
when we would, perhaps, after reading the fragment of the
third lecture, expect him to say "sacramentally and spiritually"? [35] But there are clear reasons for using the word
"virtually" with reference to the basic meaning of "virtue"
as "essential power" or "effective essence." In the third
lecture the "spiritual" receiving occurs when one attends
mass devoutly, but does not personally take the sacrament.
In More's usage one receives the sacrament "virtually" when
he receives the actual sacrament in a spiritual way. All this
is made clear by More's use of this same word "virtually"
in a passage of his *Answer to a Poisoned Book,* written a
year or so earlier. Here, in explaining the workings of the
sacrament, he speaks of "effectual receiving, by which a man
not only receiveth Christ's blessed body into his own sacramentally, but also virtually, and effectually so receiveth
therewith the spirit of God into his soul, that he is incor-
porate thereby with our Savior." [36] From this and similar
passages in the *Answer to a Poisoned Book,* we can see that
the terms *virtually, effectually,* and *spiritually* are all referring to the same essential action of the sacrament. And indeed this is clear on the second page of the treatise on the
blessed body, where More goes on to urge that we "in such
wise receive the body and blood of our Lord, as God may of
His goodness accept us for worthy, and therefore not only
enter with His blessed flesh and blood sacramentally and
bodily into our bodies, but also with His holy spirit gra-
ciously and effectually into our souls." [37]

Read in this way, the "Treatise to Receive the Blessed
Body" becomes not separate at all, but indeed the missing
treatment of the third way of receiving promised by More
at the outset of his third lecture on the sacrament. And
read thus, this section forms a most satisfying and appro-

priate conclusion to the English treatise on the Passion, for
the treatise on receiving works toward a deeper and stronger
vehemence until, in the closing page and a half, it exhorts
us to maintain the "inward speaking of Christ" in a manner that reminds one of the third and fourth books of the
Imitation of Christ. As More says, "Let us by devout prayer
talk to Him, by devout meditation talk with Him. Let us
say with the prophet: *Audiam quid loquatur in me Domi-
nus,* I will hear what our Lord will speak within me." [38]
Then the treatise on receiving closes with the example of
Zacchaeus (used also at length in the *Dialogue of Comfort*),[39] ending with a passage that provides an apt and
beautiful conclusion to the entire English treatise on the
Passion:

> With such alacrity, with such quickness of spirit, with
> such gladness, and such spiritual rejoicing, as this man re-
> ceived our Lord into his house, our Lord give us the
> grace to receive His blessed body and blood, His holy
> soul, and His almighty Godhead both, into our bodies
> and into our souls. . . . And then shall God give a gra-
> cious sentence and say upon our soul, as He said upon
> Zacchaeus: *Hodie salus facta est huic domui.* This day is
> health and salvation come unto this house: which that
> holy blessed person of Christ, which we verily in the
> blessed sacrament receive, through the merit of His bitter
> Passion (whereof He has ordained His own blessed body,
> in that blessed sacrament to be the memorial) vouchsafe,
> good Christian readers, to grant unto us all.[40]

How could this treatise on receiving the sacrament have
become detached from the remainder of the English treatise,
and been provided with a separate title, given, according to
Rastell, by More himself? Here we are utterly in the realm
of conjecture, but one might make a few suggestions. Perhaps More was interrupted in his writing and taken off to

the Tower before he had time to write this final portion of
the third lecture. Being separated from the rest of his papers, he would naturally indicate the subject of the writing
by giving it a heading, "To receive the blessed body of our
Lord, sacramentally and virtually both," in order to remind
himself or John Harris that this belonged at the end of the
other "paper that you have." Or perhaps, since this was a
matter of supreme importance, More decided to emphasize
it by giving this final portion a subtitle within the body of
the third lecture itself.[41] Standing in this way, with a separate title, the treatise could well have been interpreted to
be an entirely separate work, particularly with the reading
of that word *virtually,* which had not occurred in the earlier
part of the third lecture. In any case, I submit that the
treatise on receiving follows naturally and indeed inevitably
from the arguments that have been presented in the earlier
portion of this third lecture and in the earlier portion of
the entire English treatise on the Passion.

Furthermore, in the two manuscripts in which these treatises appear together, it is important to notice that the treatise on receiving the blessed body follows immediately *after*
the English treatise on the Passion, and not before, as it
does in the 1557 *English Works.*[42] That is to say, it is set
where I think it should be set—in between the English
treatise on the Passion and the Latin treatise. It is dealt with
as a separate treatise in both manuscripts, but nevertheless,
it is, I believe, placed in its proper position. And with the
third lecture thus completed with the climactic treatise
on receiving the sacrament, the entire English treatise on
the Passion proceeds to a satisfying conclusion.

But can we speak of such a conclusion, in view of that
very long title given to the English treatise, with its promise
to proceed as far as the sepulchre of Christ? First of all we
should note that no such long title appears in either of the
two manuscripts of this treatise.[43] And secondly, we must

remember what I have called More's art of improvisation, his art of exploratory writing. More begins with a goal, but he will not commit himself to any inflexible procedure. Consequently, as the treatise proceeds, More is free to vary and conclude as he wishes, according to interior and exterior conditions. The English treatise on the Passion, we must remember, appears to have been written, either in whole or in part, before More entered the Tower of London, and therefore, chronologically, it comes before the *Dialogue of Comfort*. Although it follows the *Dialogue* in Rastell's edition, it is not in fact the kind of meditative writing that we should expect to follow after the vehement exhortations to meditate upon the Passion that are found in the last book of the *Dialogue*. Indeed, More's English treatise on the Passion is not in any sense a meditation; it is, truly, what the repeated headings call it, a series of *lectures* in the old sense of that word: readings, interpretations, "omelies," as we read in one heading. It is a set of theological and moral sermons, expositions of the sacred text; and they have a completeness of their own.

The Latin treatise on the Passion gradually reveals itself as a work of another order and kind: a continuation, yes, a sequel, but transposed, in the musical sense, into another key. That transposition is marked by the change to another language, the language in which More wrote the most intimate writings of his that have come to us out of the Tower: those marginal annotations to the Psalms written in Latin in the Prayer Book preserved from those last days—the marginalia in which we come to the quick of More's spiritual being. Thus, as we have pointed out in the facsimile edition of the Prayer Book, certain verses from Psalm 37 form the basis for More's actions throughout all his interrogations and trial, as this marginal comment in Latin shows: "A meek man ought to behave in this way during tribulation; he should neither speak proudly himself nor retort to what

is spoken wickedly, but should bless those who speak evil
of him and suffer willingly, either for justice' sake if he
has deserved it or for God's sake if he has deserved nothing." [44]

So now, in the intimacy and sanctuary of this Latin, we
find More moving gently and gradually away from the
lecture-like manner of the English treatise and ever more
deeply into the hearing of that "inward speaking" of his
Lord, so strongly urged in the treatise on receiving which, I
think, constitutes the close of the English treatise. Throughout the Latin work we find numerous occasions, long and
short, in which the speaker hears the voice of his Redeemer
answering his meditation:

> Pluck up thy courage, faint heart, and despair never a
> deal. What though thou be fearful, sorry, and weary, and
> standest in great dread of most painful tormentry that is
> like to fall upon thee, be of good comfort for all that, for
> I myself have vanquished the whole world, and yet felt I
> far more fear, sorrow, weariness, and much more inward
> anguish too, when I considered my most bitter painful
> passion to press so fast upon me. He that is strong-hearted
> may find a thousand glorious valiant martyrs, whose en-
> sample he may right joyfully follow. But thou now, O
> timorous and weak silly sheep, think it sufficient for thee,
> only to walk after me, which am thy shepherd and gov-
> ernor; and so mistrust thyself, and put thy trust in me.[45]

These inward sayings of the Lord are answers to the personal problem raised at the outset of the Latin work, where
More draws a long and careful distinction between two
kinds of martyrs.[46] On the one hand are those who offer
their lives bravely and quickly, and on the other are those,
much more fearful, who seek to escape suffering and death,
if possible, but who ultimately are given the strength to
face death as resolutely as the more stalwart souls have done.

I am reminded of a scene in a recent movie in which
More appears, *Anne of the Thousand Days*. It is a scene in
which Fisher, the Prior of the Carthusians, and More, all
appear before Henry. Fisher and the Prior protest vehemently that the proceedings of the king are wrong and that
they will not sign the oath. Then Henry turns to More and
asks him whether he will sign, and More in a mild voice
answers, "I shall read the document with care, and hope
that my conscience will permit me to sign." At this point
the good friend with whom I attended the movie leaned
over and whispered in my ear: "Why can't More be as bold
as those other two?" It's a good question, and one that
Thomas More must often have put to himself. It is indeed
the question that underlies the entire Latin treatise on the
Passion. It is the question evoked by the Agony in the Garden and by Christ's cry, "Let this cup pass from me." More
interprets this as a scene of encouragement to the second,
faint-hearted kind of martyr, a sign that it is not wrong to
seek, as More did, all honorable and faithful methods of
escape, every loophole of the law. St. Paul himself, More
notes,

> both by policy procured to escape the Jews' deceitful
> trains through the help of a certain captain of the
> Roman garrison, and afterward got out of prison, alleg-
> ing that he was a citizen of Rome, and at another time
> saved himself from the cruel Jews by appealing unto
> Caesar, and before that, was let down over a wall in a
> basket, and so avoided the cursed hands of King Aretas.[47]

It is no sin to seek escape, so long as faith is not broken:
"Whereby it appeareth, that to fear death and torment is
none offence, but a great and grievous pain, which Christ
came not to avoid, but patiently to suffer. And we may not
by and by judge it a point of cowardness, if we see a man
either afraid and loath to be tormented, or discreetly eschew

peril in such case as he may lawfully do it." [48] There is the essence of More's position.

So the inward speaking of the Lord comes to comfort the fearful martyr, fulfilling the counsel found at the close of the *Dialogue of Comfort,* where Antony assures his nephew that meditation upon the Agony of Christ will bring the necessary comfort to sustain a Christian under the utmost threat of persecution. These three great treatises are tied together inseparably: the *Dialogue of Comfort,* the English treatise on the Passion, including as its end the treatise on receiving the sacrament, and finally, the Latin treatise. The two earlier works converge upon and prepare the way for the meditative action of the Latin work. The *Dialogue of Comfort* exhorts the reader to meditate upon the Passion, the Agony, in order to comfort the faint-hearted man, while the English treatise, in its third lecture, counsels the reader to seek interior colloquies with the Lord, saying, "And let us with Mary also sit in devout meditation, and hearken well what our Savior, being now our guest, will inwardly say unto us." [49]

Meanwhile, the Latin meditation on the Agony has a wholeness and integrity that implies a goal and design from beginning to end. That goal is plainly indicated in the title that the work bears in all three of its manuscripts, including the title arrived at after several revisions in the Valencia holograph. The treatise bears the title *De tristitia, tedio, pavore, et oratione Christi ante captionem eius,*[50] or in Mary Bassett's version: "Of the sorrow, weariness, fear, and prayer of Christ before his taking." It is not, at heart, an *Expositio:* this is an editorial title better suited to describe the English treatise. More has written here his meditations on the Agony, while he prepares his fearful soul to meet his taking. The work reaches its goal and the height of its personal application as Christ emerges from His Agony to face the approach of His captors, saying, "But this is your hour, and the power of darkness." Upon this text, near the close of the treatise, More creates his long, climactic speaking of the Lord, as Christ says to His persecutors:

> In darkness be ye, while ye ascribe my death to your own strength; and in darkness shall be your president Pilate too, as long as he shall proudly boast that he hath authority either to quit me or crucify me, who albeit mine own countrymen and bishops shall deliver me into his hands, should have no power for all that upon me, were it not given him from my Father above. And for that cause the more is their offence that shall betake me unto him. But this is your hour and the short power of darkness.[51]

We can hardly doubt that More continued these meditations to the Cross and to the Sepulchre. But this continuation perhaps existed only in the realm of mental prayer: to write it down would be too intimate a revelation for anyone to know except his Lord.

NOTES

1. *EW*, p. 1270. All quotations in this essay have been modernized.

2. *EW*, p. 1349.

3. See the account of this discovery by Geoffrey Bullough, *The Tablet*, 217 (Dec. 21, 1963): 1379–80. A facsimile of this manuscript will be published as Vol. 13, Part 2, of The Yale Edition of the Complete Works of St. Thomas More, edited by Clarence Miller, with transcription, translation, and full textual analysis.

4. *SL*, p. 188. Professor Haupt's edition of the *Treatise on the Passion*, the *Blessed Body*, and the *Devout Instructions* will appear as Vol. 13, Part 1 of the Yale edition.

5. *EW*, p. 1350. The same information is given in a note at the end of Mary Bassett's version of the Latin treatise (*EW*, p. 1404): "Sir Thomas More wrote no more of this work: for when he had written this far, he was in prison kept so strait, that all his books and pen and ink and paper was taken from him, and soon after was he put to death." See also the similar note at the end of the original printing of the work in Latin: *Opera*, Louvain, 1565, Sig. Z₁ verso.

6. A few items in this miscellany are identified as having been written before More's imprisonment: see *EW,* pp. 1418–28.

7. Rogers, No. 200.

8. Rogers, pp. 503, 505, 506; quoted from *SL,* pp. 218–19, 221, 222.

9. Rogers, No. 208.

10. Rogers, p. 536; quoted from *SL,* pp. 231–32.

11. Professor Elton questioned this statement at the Symposium, arguing that More was willing to accept Anne Boleyn as queen. But I would argue the contrary, on the basis of More's careful guarding of the conditions under which he would be willing to "swear to the succession," as indicated in More's letter to Margaret, concerning his interrogation at Lambeth. At the beginning of this letter, after he has read the "Act of the Succession," along with the oath, he says: "But as for myself in good faith my conscience so moved me in the matter that though I would not deny to swear to the succession, yet unto the oath that was offered me I could not swear, without the jubarding [i.e., jeopardizing] of my soul to perpetual damnation." Then at the close of the letter he explains again: "Surely as to swear to the succession I see no peril, but I thought and think it reason that to mine own oath I look well myself, and be of counsel also in the fashion, and never intended to swear for a pece [i.e., piece, part], and set my hand to the whole oath" (Rogers, pp. 502, 507; quoted from *SL,* pp. 217, 222). More seems to be willing to allow Parliament the right to declare the succession to the throne, since Parliament could legally settle the succession, even upon an illegitimate child of the King. But Parliament could not, it seems, in More's view, declare Anne a legitimate wife of Henry, and thus truly queen. Marriage is a matter for the church, and More's church had declared that Katherine's marriage was still intact. More's careful guarding of the conditions on which he would "swear to the succession" would seem to involve his unwillingness to recognize Anne as truly "the Queen's Grace." More refused to attend Anne's coronation. Why would he refuse, if he was willing to accept her as a true queen?

[Editor's note: after reading this footnote in galley form, Professor Elton writes as follows: "I am sure More meant Anne by the queen's grace—if Louis can't believe that More ever accepted the second marriage as valid (in which opinion he may be right), it would still be the case that Parliament had fixed not only the succession but also who should be queen. I.e., More may have believed that Henry and Anne weren't married but still felt able to call Anne queen." R.S.S.].

12. Rogers, No. 206.

13. Rogers, No. 205.

14. *EW,* p. 1434.

15. Rogers, p. 514.

16. Rogers, p. 515.

17. Rogers, p. 516.

18. Rogers, p. 517.

19. Rogers, p. 518.

20. Rogers, p. 520. But More adds: "And yet albeit that I suppose this to be true, yet believe I not even very surely, that every man so thinketh that so sayeth."

21. Rogers, pp. 528–29.

22. Rogers, p. 529.

23. Rogers, p. 532.

24. *EW*, pp. 1183–85.

25. *EW*, p. 1187: quotations from the *Dialogue of Comfort* are given according to the text prepared for the modernized edition of this treatise, to be published by the Yale University Press.

26. *EW*, p. 1179. See my essay, "The Design of More's *Dialogue of Comfort*," *Moreana* 15–16 (1967): 331–46; and Joaquin Kuhn, "The Function of Psalm 90 in Thomas More's *A Dialogue of Comfort*," *Moreana* 22 (1969): 61–67.

27. *EW*, p. 1211.

28. *EW*, pp. 1235, 1263.

29. *EW*, p. 1264.

30. *EW*, p. 1348.

31. Ibid.

32. *EW*, p. 1349.

33. *EW*, p. 1264.

34. See the reference to 1 Corinthians 11:27 in *EW*, pp. 1265, 1349.

35. For a while I pondered the idea that "virtually" might be a scribal misreading of the word "spiritually"; one can see, from examining More's handwriting, several ways in which such a misreading might have occurred. But the fact that the word "virtually" occurs three times would in itself make such an error unlikely.

36. *EW*, p. 1066. The whole of Chapter 18 in Book I of the *Answer to a Poisoned Book* helps to clarify the meaning: see *EW*, pp. 1065–68.

37. *EW*, p. 1265.

38. *EW*, p. 1268.

39. *EW*, pp. 1206–07.

40. *EW*, p. 1269.

41. As the result of a discussion at the Symposium, Clarence Miller has written to point out that the Valencia manuscript of the Latin treatise on the Passion contains two subtitles of this kind, placed in positions that might well explain the appearance of the treatise on receiving as a separate work. He writes: "The last two gatherings (F and G) of the *Expositio* begin with subsidiary titles or headings ('De amputata Malchi auricula' and 'De fuga discipulorum') which were also written on the last pages of the preceding gatherings (E and F) instead of ordinary catchwords in order to ensure the correct sequence of the gatherings. Now consider what might

have happened if gathering F (which includes all of the section
entitled 'De fuga discipulorum' and nothing but that section) had
somehow been separated from the other gatherings and the last page
of the preceding gathering (E) had been mutilated or damaged so
that the subtitle 'De fuga discipulorum' had been lost. Then gathering F, 'De fuga discipulorum,' might have been printed as a separate
short essay with its own title, like the Blessed Body." The incomplete
condition of the Royal manuscript of the English treatise on the
Passion, as described in the next note, would suggest that something
of this sort may well have occurred.

42. In the Oxford manuscript (Ms. Bodl. 431) the treatise on receiving follows after five blank pages. Then after a blank leaf follows the letter to Harris mentioned above, correcting a certain matter concerning the paschal feast. Lastly, after a blank page, follows
the Latin treatise on the Passion. This is the whole of the manuscript, which was apparently compiled to give a complete set of
More's works on the Passion.

In the British Museum manuscript (Ms. Royal 17 D XIV), the
English treatise on the Passion stops with an incomplete *second*
lecture on the sacrament; it lacks the long series of citations from
the Church Fathers. Instead, the manuscript gives directions in Latin
for providing these citations (see f. 314 verso). Were these directions
intended for John Harris? Similar directions also occur earlier in
this second lecture (see f. 302 verso, and f. 314 recto.) The fragment
of the third lecture is missing. The treatise on receiving follows on
the very next page (f. 315 recto). And the Latin treatise follows, after
a blank page.

43. Ms. Bodl. 431 has no title at all for this treatise: it begins with
the heading: "The first point, of the fall of Angels." In the Royal
Ms. the treatise is entitled simply "A Treatise upon the Passion."
Father Marc'hadour suggested to me at the Symposium that the
English treatise on the Passion really constitutes the "second part" of
the *Answer to a Poisoned Book* which More promised to write, by way
of answer to the second part of his adversary's treatise, a part dealing
with the institution of the Eucharist (see *EW*, p. 1038). This excellent
suggestion would make it plausible that More did not plan to extend
the English treatise beyond the exposition of the sacrament.

44. *Thomas More's Prayer Book: A Facsimile Reproduction of the
Annotated Pages,* ed. Louis L. Martz and Richard S. Sylvester (New
Haven, 1969), pp. xlii–xliii, 75.

45. *EW*, pp. 1357–58. See the useful modernized edition of Mary
Bassett's translation, *St. Thomas More's History of the Passion,* ed.
P. E. Hallett (London, 1941).

46. See the meditation on the text *Tristis est anima mea usque ad
mortem: EW*, pp. 1354–58.

47. *EW*, p. 1356.

48. Ibid.

49. *EW*, p. 1268.

50. This is the subtitle in the Louvain edition of 1565 (omitting the "et" before "oratione"); but the editor provides the main title: *Expositio Passionis Domini, ex Contextu Quatuor Evangelistarum usque ad Comprehensum Christum* . . . (sig. V4). Similarly, Rastell provides a main title in 1557: "An Exposition of a Part of the Passion of our Savior Jesus Christ . . ." (*EW*, p. 1350.)

Clarence Miller has also pointed out that at an early stage in the evolution of More's title the Valencia manuscript carries the heading "De oratione ante passionem christi." This would suggest that More's plan from the beginning was to concentrate upon the prayer of Christ in the Garden of Gethsemane. Considering all the manuscript evidence, Professor Miller writes, "On the whole, I tend to think that what we have is not quite finished, but very nearly so."

51. *EW*, p. 1397.

G. R. ELTON

Thomas More, Councillor

"The king's good servant, but God's first." Few of Thomas More's words are more familiar than this valediction on the scaffold. It is therefore rather strange that the many historians who have concerned themselves with his life should have paid so little attention to the first part of this self-assessment, however justified they may have been, being moved by zeal, in writing glosses on the second. Even before he became lord chancellor, More had been a member of King Henry's government for some twelve years—a third of all his adult life. Yet in Chambers' biography, typical in this as in so much else, these years occupy seventy-nine out of four hundred pages, and even of these seventy-nine at least twenty-two are concerned with More's private life. Chambers was only following the pattern set by the early biographers, from Roper onwards, who all inserted their description of More's family and friends into those years. This imbalance, produced by the desire to get on to the dramatic last phase, has left us with some important and difficult questions—just why, for instance, did Henry choose More to succeed Wolsey?—and has obscured our view of some of Sir Thomas' most active years.

Between them, More and Erasmus have succeeded in creating a firm impression that More entered the king's service with the greatest reluctance and performed his distasteful duties in a constant spirit of nostalgic regret for the joys of uncommitted scholarship. Yet he was a councillor, held several offices, served as Speaker in the Commons, and made a good deal of money out of office; he was several times involved in diplomatic negotiations; and his name appears frequently in the official correspondence of the time. If the unforeseeable disasters of the divorce and the break with Rome had not supervened, he would have lived out his days as a respected senior minister, one of the statesmen of the age of Wolsey and Gattinara. There must at least be some doubt about accounts which pay so little heed to this side of him and so manifestly arrange events with an eye to the future.

The improbabilities and errors begin right at the start of the story, with More's entry into the royal service and his appointment to the Council. There is here a conflict between ascertainable fact and contemporary comment, the second having predictably been preferred to the first. In July 1518 Erasmus told Bombasius that More had been made a councillor, and in September that year Giustiniani spoke of the appointment as though it was recent.[1] Both were aware that entry into service had preceded entry into the Council, for the Venetian knew in February that More was commissioned to act in a dispute, while Erasmus in April lamented to More himself his desertion of letters for the royal service.[2] When More visited Calais in the autumn of 1517, Erasmus clearly supposed that he was not yet of the Council; and Professor Hexter therefore dates the entry into service into the first quarter of 1518.[3] All this is much too late, as the commissions for More's embassies testify. Two were issued for the one to Flanders which produced *Utopia*. The first is unhelpful, but the second, of October 2, 1515, distinguishes between Cuthbert Tunstal and William Knight, called "our councillors," and Sir Thomas Spinelli, John Clifford (governor of the merchant adventurers) and

Thomas More, who are not so described. On the other hand, the commission for Calais, dated August 26, 1517 gives the councillor's title to all the commissioners—Sir Richard Wingfield, Knight, and More.[4] By this date, therefore, More was sworn of the Council. Whether he was at some earlier date already formally in the king's service, it is impossible to say. Envoys were normally in that position, which was formal, not casual, but exceptions certainly occurred. The 'dialogue of counsel' in *Utopia* (to use Hexter's description), between More and Hythloday, written in the late summer of 1516, has always been read as describing his inner debate whether to accept the call. Hexter has also noted, very perceptively, that in his defense of entry into the Council the fictional More for once gets the better of his humanist self,[5] which suggests the possibility that the decision may already have been taken. At any rate, by August 1517 More was a councillor. Yet Erasmus, whose correspondence with More remained frequent and regular, clearly stayed ignorant of this fact for the best part of a year. The record leaves no doubt of this, and it calls for a reassessment of More's behavior.

The story of More's councillor's fee bears out these implications. In the end he got an annuity of £100, the usual retainer for the king's Council. The first mention of a pension occurs in a letter from More to Erasmus of February 17, 1516, in which he described his financial difficulties, "even though," he says, "on my return the king granted me an annuity, and this is manifestly not to be despised, whether one looks to the honor or the profit."[6] But he added that he would probably refuse the money because it would conflict with his office as undersheriff of London: if he were feed by the king, he might not be thought impartial in defending the privileges of the City. Although this annuity was seemingly never paid, the one that was casts doubt upon the general supposition that his reasons for refusing in 1516 were not those he gave but rather a wider reluctance to enter the king's service. On June 21, 1518, he was granted £100 a year, backdated to Michaelmas 1517 and payable partly out of the Exchequer of Receipt and partly in assignments on the petty custom of London.[7] In practice, he was to receive half from each source, and the payments were made fairly regularly thereafter, on the authority of a patent enrolled in the Exchequer in the Michaelmas Term 1518. He never had long to wait for his money, at least half of which he got in cash, not tallies, and he was especially favored on occasion by receiving tallies on sources of revenue different from those specified in the patent.[8]

The really surprising thing is the document which authorized the patent under which he was paid. If More had been as reluctant to accept the fee as is commonly stated, giving way only to pressure from the king, one would have expected a signet letter, the usual instrument for expressing the king's initiative. Instead one finds a signed bill, that is a petition from the grantee, in standard form, which the king's signature turned into a warrant for the great seal. The king signed on June 21, and the bill was at once delivered into Chancery: in this speed, and in the bypassing of the lesser seals, there is a measure of favor. But the document makes it plain that the initiative came from More, and there is really no reason to question it. I have never found cause to doubt that such signed petitions meant exactly what they said, and since Henry had other often-used instruments at his disposal if he was really engaged in forcing a fee upon More in order to tie him to his service, I am compelled to accept that, on the contrary, More had to petition for the money. The backdating of payment by nine months supports this view. It looks as though More was promised his fee in mid-1517, when he was first appointed to the Council, but then waited patiently and in vain for the king to act, until in the end he had to draw Henry's attention to the fact that nothing had been done.

Thus More was a councillor long before he allowed Erasmus to know as much, and had to take steps to get the money attached to the place. This hardly suggests the reluctance to enter office which has always been ascribed to him. Indeed, what evidence is there for all this reluctance? In *Utopia* he discusses the pros and cons, but, as we have seen, he puts up a very good case for accepting. His own stated reasons for refusing a pension had nothing to do with doubts about office. He had been a judicial officer of London since 1510. He was trained as a common lawyer, a man in close contact with government—incidentally, a background very different from that of all his humanist friends. The most explicit evidence for his distaste for office comes not from himself but from Erasmus who told Hutten in 1519 that the king had had to drag More into court since "no one ever strove more energetically to get court appointment than More endeavoured to avoid it," a point repeated a year later in a letter to Brixius in which More's exceptional qualities are said to have forced the king not to rest until he had dragged him (*pertraxerit*) into his inmost counsels.[9] More's own occasional comments on the horrors of court life and his preference for books or the company of his family are no more than the conventional—and conventionally sincere—talk of the intellectual involved in the absurdities of a public existence. These feelings got into the early biographies, as in Roper's pleasant story of More hiding his wit in order to get away from Henry's drawn-out supper parties.[10] When More told Fisher, soon after the decisive step had been taken, that everybody knew his unwillingness to attend court (and that Henry himself was in the habit of twitting him about it) [11] he was no doubt telling the truth, but not all the truth, for his place at court (as we shall see) was soon absorbing enough. There really is no evidence at all that he lived twelve years against the grain, and he followed Henry's call at so early a date that he cannot have hesitated long. But he did not like to admit all this to Erasmus, so much so that he allowed him to suppose that no decision had been taken even while, as king's councillor, he was negotiating at Calais and expecting Erasmus to visit. More, it would seem, respected Erasmus' known opposition to a scholar's involvement in affairs sufficiently to prevaricate about his own contrary view. Yet despite Erasmus' occasional disgust at the loss to letters, he did to some extent take his friend's point: better a More in attendance upon that good humanist monarch, King Henry VIII, than the common run of councillors.[12] On the other hand, he soon reverted to a more normal attitude when in June 1521 he regretted, to Pace, More's advance in service: "he is doing so well at court that I am sorry for him." [13] More's earlier silence rested on a correct apprehension—in both senses of that word—of the great man's feelings about princely courts.

At any rate, in trying to understand More's place in government, we should abandon the conventional talk about his reluctance to enter it. He went with his eyes open; he meant to make a career; the story of his fee suggests that he was not stupidly averse to gaining some profit. In short, his entry into the Council was a serious matter, not the act of a man pulling faces privately at those with whom he worked publicly.

The official record of More's activities as councillor is not impressive. Of the twenty-five Council meetings of which evidence survives during the time of his membership, he attended only five;[14] even his father, the judge, did better with seven. In part, no doubt, this reflects the bias of the evidence which consists of transcripts concen-

trating on the Council's judicial activities, but the fact
also suggests something important about the real meaning of More's part in government. Routine Council sessions were not for him. It is not even clear whether he
was present in the Star Chamber as late as February 1528
when a dispute was committed to him, the chief baron
and two lawyers: his fellow commissioners were certainly
not there.[15] On the other hand, he from the first under-
took work which suggests an inferior place in the official
hierarchy but a meaningful place in the personal entourage, as when, in April 1518, he was seeing to the medi-
cal precautions for the court as it moved to Woodstock.[16]
He took his share in the familiar legal councillor's work
of putting Crown debtors under bond.[17] None of this
signifies much or indicates what the king might have
wanted him for. Roper says that he was made master of
requests because nothing better was available at first.[18]
No such office formally existed at the time, but More was
certainly among the councillors detailed to hear poor
men's complaints in one of the committees from which
the real court was to spring, though the extant signs of
his work are few. In January 1519 he signed a commission out of the court, and at some unknown date he personally endorsed on a bill the order for a privy seal of
appearance.[19] He seems, in fact, to have been joined with
one of the really active Requests councillors, Dr. John
Clerk, then dean of the Chapel Royal, an officer who at
this time specialized in hearing these kinds of pleas. In
October 1519 they shared a mess in the Household and
worked together on some obscure business. A little later
More shared a breakfast allowance with John Stokesley,
the almoner and the other leading judge in Requests
matters.[20] It almost looks as though the later practice of
linking civilians in Requests with at least one common
lawyer had already started, and as though More filled

that place for some two years. It all amounts to saying
that his was a very lowly start in the Council; clearly, his
assurance to Fisher that he stood "a long way from the
king's close favor" was true enough.[21]

The moment of prosperity, which called forth Erasmus'
dark suspicions, came with his knighthood and appointment as undertreasurer of the Exchequer. This happened
in May 1521, nearly four years after his first entry into
the Council.[22] According to Erasmus, he neither sought
nor petitioned for the office, and the king preferred him
to another good candidate who was willing to pay for it.[23]
Perhaps: at any rate, if More was ever to make a career, it
was high time for him to get something of value. The
undertreasurer deputized for the lord treasurer in the
Lower Exchequer. He supervised and coordinated the
officials responsible for receiving and disbursing money
and those engaged in the Lower Exchequer's chief formal
activity, the production of tallies. In addition he had custody of the Treasury of the Receipt, the government's
chief archive for treaties and other diplomatic documents.
He possessed neither place nor authority in the Upper
Exchequer, where the accounts were taken, or in the Exchequer of Pleas where revenue cases were heard; the
office thus fell somewhat short of the splendor which
Erasmus, who confused it with the lord treasureship
proper, supposed to attach to it.[24] Nevertheless, it was a
very real step up. How heavy its duties were cannot be
estimated. The undertreasurer put his name to the annual 'Declarations of the State of the Treasury' rendered
by the Receipt, but the work of preparing them naturally
fell to the officers under his control.[25] No doubt he
checked the statements, for which he was responsible, before letting them go forward. On one occasion, Henry had
to do without More's attendance because some settling
of accounts required his presence at the Exchequer.[26] He

was personally involved on several occasions when documents in the Treasury were signed out in the course of diplomatic negotiations.[27] Manifestly, he attended to the routine duties of the office. To all appearance, these were not overwhelming; and there is not the slightest sign that his tenure included anything of interest in the history of either Thomas More or the Exchequer.

Perhaps another of Erasmus' remarks explains why More was offered and accepted an office for which nothing in his previous career had qualified him. Erasmus told both Pace and Budé, in identical words, that More's new appointment carried a "far from disagreeable salary." [28] The salary was £173 6s. 8d., easily the second highest paid in the whole of the Exchequer. Only the lord treasurer's £365 exceeded it; even the chief baron got only £100. More's principal subordinate in the Receipt, the writer of the tallies who as auditor of the Receipt was from about 1554 onwards to take over the undertreasurer's functions, had to be satisfied with £41 13s. 4d.[29] The undertreasurership was thus an exceptionally valuable office—light duties, and a remarkably high salary. The stipend probably reflects the fact that, unlike the active officers of the Receipt, the undertreasurer was not in the way of earning additional regular fees. He performed no services for individual clients of the Exchequer, and the chances are that More got just his official salary from the office. But that was a real plum.

On September 30, 1525,[30] More exchanged the office for the chancellorship of the Duchy of Lancaster, an appointment much more suited to his training and abilities since its main function was that of an equity judge. His predecessor, Sir Richard Wingfield, who on July 22 had died at Toledo, on embassy to Spain, had been one of the king's most trusted councillors.[31] The chancellor of the Duchy received a salary of £66 13s. 4d. and, in addition, 'wages' at 6s. 8d. a day for the time spent attending the court of Duchy Chamber. This time had become conventionalized at eighty-four days in the year, making a further payment of £28.[32] In the year ending Michaelmas 1525, the salary—or rather, since he died in the middle of the year, £50 of it—went to Wingfield; More had none of it, and it was presumably deliberate economy that delayed his appointment to the beginning of the financial year. On the other hand, More got the £28 wages for the year preceding his entry upon office, which suggests that he possibly already carried out its duties during Wingfield's absence. From Michaelmas 1525 till he vacated the office in October 1529 he was paid the full £94 13s. 4d., a markedly smaller income than that which the undertreasurership had yielded. However, it is quite certain that the chancellor was entitled to a share in the Duchy's sealing fees; for these, no account survives. More's tenure of this office is at present being studied by Miss Margaret Hastings, and I will not therefore pursue the point here any further; but it is already clear that he attended to what for a change were quite arduous duties with his customary conscientiousness.

More obtained one other office in this decade when, in 1523, he was elected Speaker of the House of Commons, at this time effectively a government appointment. The truth is underlined by the well-known story of Wolsey's exasperation which, Roper tells us, made him regret the day that he had More made Speaker. As usual, he did his duty by securing the much-needed subsidy against strong opposition, and he made his mark in parliamentary history by the striking plea for freedom of speech which he included in his petition for privileges. The story is too familiar to need re-telling here.[33] In itself, however, the Speakership testifies only to his favor with king and cardinal, and to his general standing among the gentle-

men of England. Like the rest of his offices, it makes no
particular sense in terms of an official career. More ac-
quired places as they happened to fall vacant and were
bestowed on him, it seems, as marks of respect and by
way of gradual elevation. None of them gave him administrative responsibilities of the first order, none bestowed political power, and he never held more than one
at a time.

More's incoherent career in office underlines another
strange aspect of his service to the Crown. He fits none of
the standard categories of royal officers. There were essentially three ways in which men trained for such ca-
reers—the ways of the courtier, the bureaucrat and the
lawyer. A man might rise either through the hierarchy
of the king's personal entourage, or by working in the
executive agencies, or as legal counsel (lay or spiritual)
involved in protecting the king's rights in the courts. Of
course, the three roads were not always perfectly separate:
Sir Reginald Bray, for instance, who had been primarily
an administrator, also attended to the work of a Crown
lawyer and, at the dull court of Henry VII, counted for
something of a courtier too. Nevertheless, it is usually possible to assign the servants of Tudor kings to one of these
three categories. With Thomas More this cannot be done.
Henry liked to have him around, in which sense he was
a courtier: on one occasion he could be listed in the es-
tablishment of the Chamber.[34] His work in Council and
Exchequer placed him with the administrators. His training and previous experience, on the other hand, cast him
most obviously for the role of legal counsel. If the courtier
careerist may be exemplified (as indeed he may) by the
likes of Sir William Compton or Sir Nicholas Carew, the
highly unmilitary and subfusc Sir Thomas More hardly
fits the stereotype. The greatest of the administrators to
reach high office was Thomas Cromwell, as different from

More in background and use of office as can be imagined, but quite typical of his category of royal servant. And as legal counsel, More was not even a patch on his father who ended up as a judge (the proper culmination of that career) and frequently sat in the king's Council in that capacity. "Office" thus hardly describes Sir Thomas's place in the government of England.

On the other hand, office gave him a necessary income. The legend endows More with a total indifference to cash; the facts, more sensibly, show that he made a reasonable thing out of his service. If Roper is right in saying that on entering the king's service More gave up £400 a year from private practice, he needed some recompense. From Michaelmas 1517 to his arrest, at Easter 1534, he received the £100 annuity attached to his councillorship. He did very well to obtain the highly paid undertreasurership, and he is not likely to have lost much, if anything, by exchanging it for the Duchy. Unlike some, he recovered the costs of his embassies.[35] He does not figure largely as a recipient of patronage, but he is not absent from the list. Lands he never went after, though in May 1522 he did acquire the manor of South, in Kent, out of the Buckingham forfeiture,[36] and he obtained two wardships—the valuable one of Sir John Heron's heir Giles (whom he married to one of his daughters) and that of John Moreton, a lunatic.[37] His most valuable grant was a licence of June 1526 to export 1000 woollen cloths, a characteristic gift to a courtier who was expected to exploit it by selling it on to an actual cloth-exporter, as More no doubt did.[38] These are not large pickings, but neither are they negligible. There are also signs that he got the windfalls and private pensions which came to men of influence. As soon as his standing at court was assured, he found himself 'retained of council' by Westminster Abbey, a body good at spotting winners; this notional employment was worth 20s. a year to him.[39] As one of the negotiators of the Treaty of the More (1525), he shared in the pensions bestowed by Francis I to the tune of 150 crowns (about £35) a year,[40] and once he was chancellor of the Duchy he got on the gravy train supplied by men of substance who wished to buy favor through regular retainers. In December 1527, Bishop West bestowed on him the keepership of Hatfield Park, a sinecure worth 40s. a year plus customary dues.[41] Lord Darcy also paid him 40s. a year, and the earl of Northumberland, desperate for friends, gave him the very large annual fee of £21.[42] Since none of More's private accounts survive, we cannot tell how many more people acted similarly. The system of attaching interest at the center by modest annuities was general—Darcy and Northumberland happen to have left private record of their purposeful munificence. It is more likely that this represents a minimum than that no one else recognized More's standing in the usual way.

More's total income cannot be calculated, but he clearly did well enough. A subsidy assessment of 1527 puts him very high among those included in the king's Chamber, a repository of acquisitive wealth. At £340 a year in lands and fees (in his case, of course, mostly fees since the councillor's annuity and the duchy stipend amounted to nearly £200 a year) he was topped only by such notoriously greedy courtiers as Compton, Sir Francis Brian and Richard Weston.[43] No one wants to suggest that More was secretly avaricious: the fact that he evidently did not use his position to exploit the king's bounty more frequently testifies to his essential restraint. However, he was by no means above the rewards of office, a point he proved in connection with the Speakership. Wolsey may have worked off some annoyance on him, but immediately after the end of the session he wrote to the king, suggesting that More had deserved the customary reward of £100 paid in the past over and above the Speaker's fee, which amounted to the same sum. The cardinal added a touch of personal kindness: he was taking the initiative because Sir Thomas "is not the most ready to speake and solicit his own cause." [44] Sir Thomas was very properly grateful when the king complied, but he knew the situation well enough to urge Wolsey to write specially to the treasurer of the Chamber so that the money, allocated there, would actually be paid when he sent for it.[45] The Parliament had been a hard one, but £200 was not a bad reward for some seventeen weeks' work.

Service to the king provided a good living, but that had not been More's purpose in entering it. The history of More's offices, and of his activities in them, shows that neither the good living nor the routine administration involved reflect his intentions in entering the Council— or the king's intentions in placing him there. What then was he doing, at court, in Council, and day by day? An analysis of the surviving evidence shows that two types of activity occupied him most fully. He was much engaged in diplomatic negotiations, and he spent a great deal of time acting as a kind of secretary to Henry.

Diplomacy had first revealed his capacity to the king, and he remained one of the men whom Wolsey employed in the conduct of his foreign policy. It is not, in fact, too easy to sort out More's various negotiations from the accounts given by his biographers, ancient or modern, but it seems clear that in this matter, as in his holding of office, he worked his way up from a relatively lowly position to one of modest prominence. At the start, he took part only in commercial negotiations, as became a citizen and official of London. His visit to Calais in August–November 1517, when he was very much the junior envoy by the side of Wingfield and Knight, was mainly concerned with a dispute between English and French merchants there.[46] In February 1518 an obscure business over wines, involving the Venetian ambassador, was about to be committed to Pace and himself, though it does not look as though anything came of this.[47] In 1520 he was of the company that went with the king to the Field of Cloth of Gold, an experience which surprisingly seems to have left no echo among the reminiscences of his public life which he scattered through his various writings; on this occasion, too, matters of commerce provided his only employment when he was in a commission appointed to negotiate with the merchants of the German Hanse.[48] The discussions adjourned to Bruges where he followed Wolsey as the cardinal moved from the serious business of the Calais junketings to the frivolities of alliance-making with Charles V. On the first occasion he was the third of four commissioners, on the second the second of six; on both he talked more than anyone else and clearly acted as spokesman—as the Germans noted, the Englishmen replied "Moro verbum faciente." [49] He impressed the other side by his use of "the soft speech and calm demeanor customary among the English." [50] But the commissioners were not very high-powered—men of business rather than men of ambassadorial rank—and so far, at least, More occupied a distinctly minor place in the diplomatic service. At the same time, the Hanseatic reports leave a clear impression of skill and reasonable success.

When his chance came he turned it down, begging to be excused from the embassy to Spain in 1525. There is no reason to believe Roper, who thought the offer a plot of Wolsey's to get rid of a displeasing critic; [51] if More had been interested in a normal diplomatic career, the appointment would have marked a genuine promotion and been welcome. As it was, his luck held at this time. His replacement, Sir Richard Wingfield, died inconti-

nently upon arrival in Spain, and More not only inherited
the chancellorship of the Duchy but stepped into the va-
cancy among the king's ambassadorial personnel. His first
major employment followed close upon his refusal of
Spain when, with Nicholas West, bishop of Ely, he engaged in the discussions which resulted in the important
Treaty of the More (August 1525)—the treaty by which
Wolsey announced his shift from an imperial to a French
alliance after the emperor's triumph at Pavia.[52] More
alone signed the draft of the treaty, but when the formal
instrument came to be signed his name appears last of a
list of nine, to testify to his continued inferiority in the
official hierarchy.[53] Henceforth he remained reasonably active in such matters, engaged in an agreement with the
French envoy de Vaux in August 1525, as one of the
English commissioners for the treaty of April 1527 which
preceded Wolsey's embassy to France in July that year
(an embassy which included More),[54] and finally joined
with Tunstal as envoys to the negotiations at Cambrai
in mid-1529 when the peace between Charles V and
Francis I destroyed Wolsey's foreign policy and in effect
the cardinal as well.[55] Cambrai was a diplomatic disaster
for England and for Henry VIII, but the blame fell on
Wolsey, not on the two diplomatists who had been appointed over his head. They fared well: Tunstal was, in
1530, promoted from London to Durham, and More, of
course, returned from Cambrai to find himself pressed
to accept the great seal. Roper reckoned that this offer
of the highest office in the land in part reflected the king's
satisfaction with Sir Thomas's skill in his recent embassy.[56] Perhaps: though no one, not even More, could
or did save anything from the wreck of the Ladies' Peace,
and (as we shall see) there may have been better reasons
for this striking promotion.

Thus, from 1525 More came to be one of the leading

experts in foreign policy, though never until the last occasion (when Wolsey no longer controlled appointments)
given first-class standing. He achieved some prominence
in the king's entourage when Henry received ambassadors:
in November 1526 he welcomed the new orator of Venice
with a prepared speech in reply to an address of which
Wolsey had thoughtfully obtained a copy three days in
advance, and six months later he was again in attendance
when Secretary Dodieu had an audience with the king.[57]
His knowledge of languages and of Europe, his reputation
for uprightness and fair dealing,[58] his notorious ability
to keep his own counsel, all seemed to cast him for the
diplomatic service. It looks as though he was treated as
something of a specialist in French affairs. But in all this
activity he was never anything but an agent, and there
is no sign at all that he influenced policy. Since most of
his activities took place in England and none took him
far afield, he never achieved that distance from Wolsey
which forced policy-making decisions upon so many ambassadors at this time of slow communications. No doubt
the king was pleased with him, but could he himself be
pleased with this tedious and uninfluential position? His
work in foreign affairs explains neither his continued
service nor his sudden elevation, nor does it justify his
reputation. Many others looked far more important. The
real secret of More's career lies closer to the heart of government than this.

As the record makes very plain, from first entering the
king's service More remained very near to the king's person. Erasmus' constant use of "court" as equivalent to
"office" is in More's case absolutely correct. In fact, though
he never held the principal secretaryship, he was effectively
a second or substitute secretary.[59] Wolsey recognized this
as early as August 1518 when he used Pace (principal
secretary) and More indifferently and jointly to communi-

cate the latest news to Henry.[60] Henry himself played a
variant on this theme in the following February: wishing
to bestow a preferment in Tunstal's gift on Pace, he told
More, in the beneficiary's presence, to write the necessary
letter of request.[61] From the middle of 1519 onwards,
there survives a regular series of letters showing More as
intermediary between cardinal and king. More, accom-
panying the king's progress, reports Henry's special favor
to the city of Waterford (always loyal), relates Henry's
pleasure at Wolsey's good health (which his highness is
pleased to ascribe to his own advice to avoid medicine),
conveys instructions for diplomatic dispatches to be written by Wolsey, possibly with a sense of pleasure passes on
Henry's smug reminder that he had always distrusted the
cardinal of Sion and told Wolsey so—"wherby he thinketh your Grace will the bettre truste his coniecture hereafter." [62] At this time, Secretary Pace was in Germany
and More had taken his place. The continental travels
of 1520–21 intervened, and More's standing with the
king grew, till in July 1521 Pace found himself writing
to Wolsey:

> The Kynge signifieth Your Grace that where as old
> men doith nowe decaye gretly within thys Hys realme,
> hys mynde is to aqwaynte other yonge men wyth hys
> grette affayris, and therfore he desyrith Your Grace to
> make Sir Wyllyam Sandys, and Syr Thomas More,
> priveye to all such matiers as your Grace schall treate
> at Calice.[63]

More was forty-three, Sandys at least thirty-five (and
Wolsey forty-six)—but still: Sir Thomas's star seemed as-
cendant.

Yet so far as the evidence goes, his standing remained
much the same, or at any rate, such growth of influence
and importance as one can discern was no quicker than

would be justified by the familiarity and experience which the years were bound to bring. The correspondence with Wolsey resumes in 1521 and continues steadily for some three years. All of it is distinctly official but intimate. More gets involved in searching the rolls (in company with his father and Serjeant Brooke) to find precedents for the appointment of the Deputy of Ireland; fortunately, he can agree with Wolsey's view of the matter.[64] The minute Pace is off again on diplomatic missions, More acts in effect as secretary, getting the king's signature on papers, reading Wolsey's letters to him, conveying his instructions. He apologizes for his failure to send a copy of Henry's letter to the lord steward, being forced to summarize it from memory because Henry had had it dispatched before it could be copied.[65] He takes the opportunity to flatter Wolsey on his "moost politiquely and moste prudently devised" letters,[66] and gets even more expansive when conveying the king's deep appreciation of Wolsey's "labor, studie, payn and travaile" in dealing so speedily with matters "whan the onely redyng therof held hym aboue twoo howris." [67] The letters frequently record effusive thanks: More knew how Wolsey, always jealous and suspicious of the king's secretaries, should be written to. Between August and November 1523, when Wolsey was at Westminster, the king on progress, and Pace in Italy about the succession to Pope Adrian VI, there survive thirteen letters which display More as intermediary between the king and his minister. But not one shows him doing anything more than receive and transmit orders and information in both directions: there is no single note of independent intervention. He had shown more of that (in a very small matter) in October 1522 when, ordered to write a sharp letter to the Earl of Arundel on Sir Arthur Poole's behalf, he successfully suggested that a loving letter be tried first.[68]

After 1523 few such letters of More's survive, but Wolsey certainly continued to use him as his link with the king. More's constant attendance upon his sovereign was manifest, and Vives thought that thanks to it it would be easy to arrange a visit from Erasmus.[69] After all, as early as June 1522, thinking himself insufficiently attended, Henry had asked that others besides Sir Thomas be detached from Wolsey's entourage and attached to his own.[70] Nor did the elevation to the chancellorship of the Duchy make any immediate difference: More was still employed in reading Wolsey's letters to the king.[71] His standing, however, improved somewhat. In September 1526, Pace's successor William Knight (who eight years earlier had clearly outranked More) dared not presume to open letters addressed to Sir Thomas in the latter's temporary absence on the king's business, though More kindly returned the dispatch and asked Knight to act for him.[72] He was now a man of weight whose opinion was required to execute Wolsey's design of a proclamation, though if he were not to return in time Sir William Fitzwilliam would do instead, as the only other "of the hed officers" present.[73] But business had to go on, and a few days later Knight overcame his diffidence sufficiently to open a letter addressed to More so as to read it to the king.[74]

From 1519 to late 1526, More was in effect the king's spare secretary; thereafter he rarely acted in this capacity, and since the date roughly coincides with his promotion in office the evidence of the extant correspondence is likely to be correct, not the product of accidental survival. Certainly all this put him at the center of affairs, in the secret activities of government. For instance, he got involved in one of Wolsey's more dubious maneuvers when, in February 1525, the cardinal decided to intercept the imperial ambassador's dispatches. The way Wolsey told

it to Richard Sampson, then in Spain, a messenger had
been arrested on suspicion by the ordinary watch at
Brentford; the letters found on him were taken to the
solicitor general, who passed them to More, who sent
them next morning to Wolsey, then sitting in court in
the Chancery. In Spain they said that More had been
responsible for the illegal arrest, though in Brussels they
affected to believe Wolsey's story of an accident.[75] On
another occasion, More was accused by Knight of respon-
sibility for a muddle: More told Knight that he was to
attend on the Burgundian ambassadors but failed to add
that they had already arrived, so that they had unsatis-
factory entertainment.[76] It looks, in fact, as though Knight
himself had been at fault and was passing the buck.

More was certainly one of the important cogs in the
less formal sector of government—the circle round Henry
and Wolsey involved in the execution of inner policy—
and he was still, by the mid-twenties, one of the most
regular attenders at court. His peculiar position, which
owed nothing to office, was summed up in Wolsey's great
Household ordinance of January 1526, the Eltham Ordinance, in which four persons were made permanent attenders upon his majesty (or at least two of them at any
time): John Clerk, the bishop of Bath who had earlier
been dean of the Chapel, the present dean (Richard
Sampson), the secretary (William Knight), and Sir Thomas
More.[77] These men formed the upper royal secretariat of
the 1520s. The first three were clerics and official career-
ists, men specifically trained for the job and holding ap-
propriate offices. More stood among them as a freak.
Neither experience, nor appointment, nor ambition made
him a natural among the king's secretaries. But there he
was; and he must have owed a position, which cannot be
called elevated or obviously agreeable to his cast of mind,
to his personal qualities and the king's special desires.

Yet, whether he liked the place or not, and whether in the eyes of the world it stood high or not, inevitably such proximity to the king and such constant involvement in great affairs carried influence.

How much influence? His friends thought from the first that it was great. Erasmus spoke of him as "totus . . . aulicus, Regi semper assistens, cui est a secretis," as early as April 1518,[78] and Fisher in 1521, seeking his help in the interests of the University of Cambridge, was sure that someone "Regi tam intimus effectus" would be able to do a lot.[79] In reply, More questioned his influence with the king with whom, he said, he could assuredly do little.[80] So far as the evidence goes, this assessment of the situation continued to be true right down to 1529. In all those exchanges between Henry, Wolsey and More, there is no sign whatsoever that Sir Thomas ever contributed to the making of policy or tried to get his views heard. As secretary and as diplomatist he was an executor, or a channel of communication, no more. He never even offered advice to Wolsey, and the only personal touches (his formal thanks to the cardinal apart) occurred when he was transmitting explicit instructions from the king. Even in matters of patronage, a sound barometer, his voice was rarely heard and more rarely effective. Perhaps he was too straightforward for such things. In 1528, as chancellor of the Duchy, he was about to lease some property to Roger Wigston which the king wanted to go to Sir John Russell. Although Wolsey was asked to intervene on Russell's behalf, More adhered to his first intention, and the king was displeased.[81]

Why, indeed, was the king ever pleased to have More so constantly near him? What did he want from him? We know from Roper that he enjoyed More's wit and conversation. But in 1529 he made him lord chancellor: that is, he demonstrated that he had gained a high opinion of

More's sense, wisdom and competence. No doubt he had observed these qualities in More's discharge of his daily secretarial tasks, and no doubt he received advice from him in the course of their intimacy of which the record shows nothing. Yet it remains true that no sort of significant influence can be traced in the decade; there is not the slightest sign that policy, firmly in the hands of Wolsey and Henry, was ever affected by anything that More did or said, nor has anyone ever suggested that it was. He may have spoken in Council, but in those years the Council rarely met to discuss policy, and More's record of attendance (so far as the pitiful evidence goes) is not, as we have seen, impressive. The only tale remembered of words spoken in Council is of no importance: how he opposed Wolsey's plan to create a permanent office of constable in England and drew the cardinal's rude annoyance upon himself.[82] Ten years "a secretis" to Henry VIII, and so little to show for it. Just what did More mean to his king?

The only specific thing in which More assisted Henry in a more than routine capacity touched the controversy with Luther. Henry certainly discussed his book on the sacraments with More, though there need no longer be any doubt that he wrote it himself; and it is possibly true that More—as he related later—tried to warn the king against too unquestioning a support of papal claims.[83] Nevertheless, More was specifically commissioned to reply to Luther's answer, a task which enabled him to display unexpected powers of vituperation. These engagements underline what seems to me the outstanding and revealing fact: More was to be Henry's tame humanist. The king enjoyed his company and conversation, kept him close to his person, and when the occasion offered exploited his intellectual gifts and his pen. Henry liked to have intellectuals around him; he took pleasure in talking

about their concerns, and his interest in books and writers was genuine, though haphazard. For obvious reasons
he distrusted politicians and men on the make, however
freely he employed them; when he wished to relax he
turned to men like More and Cranmer who were not forever watching opportunities or plotting personal ad-
vancement. With such men, his relationship was more
personal than usual: one may speak of friendship. But
all the signs indicate that he rarely gave them political
power or relied on their advice in affairs. The fact is
notorious about Cranmer, and we have not been able to
discover any evidence that More's close relations with
Henry in the 1520s ever permitted him to influence policy.
More was Henry's pledge of Renaissance excellence, his
intellectual courtier.

That this position did not satisfy Sir Thomas is hardly
surprising. He had accepted office, with all the time-con-
suming attendance at court and the likely corruption of
public life which he let Hythloday describe in *Utopia,*
because he had become convinced that the scholar must,
if pressed, take his learning and wisdom into the service
of princes. His career was very far from meteoric, and his
offices remained unspectacular. And though he was always near the king, his tasks there seemed to be confined
to reading and writing the royal correspondence; and
however much he talked things over with Henry, he
could not see that he produced any effect upon events.
While Wolsey ruled, and with a man as devious as Henry
VIII, little political profit could derive from such intimacy, and More's well-known assessment of the king's
friendship shows how fully he understood the position.
And clearly he fretted against these pointless occupations,
until his energies found more congenial employment in
his concern for what was happening in the church. So far
as I know, More showed no special interest in Luther and

the new heresies until Henry asked him to write the refutation of Luther's attack on himself, but More's involvement thereafter is plainly documented. About 1525 he
struggled for William Roper's soul during its temporary
apostasy, his mind turned more and more to the threat
of heresy, and in March 1528 he got Tunstal's licence to
study heretical books.[84] Even before this, in January 1527,
he conducted a most surprising police raid on the Steelyard in search of vernacular bibles and Lutheran writings; he led the large company which broke in upon the
Germans after supper, allegedly by Wolsey's orders, and
when nothing incriminating was found he took the trouble to return next day to issue ominously worded demands
for the surrender of anything hidden.[85] He was turning
to new tasks and equipping himself for them. The humanist scholar had been frustrated by his decision to enter the
royal service; the royal servant by his master's manifest
refusal to go beyond personal friendship to political dependence. A man of More's stature could hardly rest content with secretarying for the king, talking to second-rank
envoys, giving judgment in the Duchy court, and amus-
ing Henry's leisure hours. Heresy, as it were, came to the
rescue, and from late 1528 onwards More presented himself to the world as England's leading controversialist
against Luther and Luther's English followers.

Of course, More's horror of heresy and his conviction
that it needed to be exterminated were perfectly genuine.
But so was his need for employment. He had sacrificed
much in 1517 when he had accepted the king's invitation
to become a councillor, as the fame and the disapproval
of Erasmus were ever-present to remind him. Was he to
have given up the pleasures of scholarship and the family
life he loved for the dust and ashes of a favorite's place
without influence? Perhaps the More of tradition would
not have worried over this sort of thing, or would simply

have sought better uses for his time. The More of tradition bore all the accidents of fortune with a balanced, stoical amusement and prepared himself for the sainthood which posterity was to bestow. But this More of tradition seems to me some distance from the real More of the 1520s.

What do we really know about Thomas More, at least before those last years when everything, including the man, had changed? We have the testimony of his circle of learned friends, which is obviously perfectly sound so far as it goes; and we have the testimony of William Roper, manifestly in awe of his formidable father-in-law even while he loved him, who wrote his book late in life and with both eyes fixed firmly on the need to present the figure of human perfection which More's terrible end demanded. Yet there is also evidence that does not fit the conventional picture too well. That More had the instincts of a scholar and loved the company of scholars is surely true, but it does not seem to me that he was one with Erasmus and Budé, Reuchlin and Lefèvre; at least, not until the needs of controversy turned him into a competent theologian. Rather was he that familiar figure, the man of affairs who was also a man of letters, though unlike most of his kind he produced one work of genius. Very likely he was aware of the distinction, for his reaction to attacks by better scholars and worse men was characteristically petulant and fierce. The amount of touchy vanity which he displayed in his quarrel with Germain de Brie astonished Miss Routh and—more important—distressed Erasmus.[86] As William Ross, defending Henry VIII against Luther, he matched Dr. Martin in violence of abuse, a remarkable achievement. His controversial manners were bad: in his exchanges with Tyndale, he generally proved the more scurrilous of the two, and he was savage to St. German who had not been savage at all.[87] The tone of his writing changed only at the end: the *Apology* suggests that he was recovering his balance, and the *Dialogue of Comfort* testifies to the serenity which came to him in his last adversity. But during his career as a controversialist he was one of the most intolerant and unfair of writers. Nor will it do to pass this off with remarks about the customs of the age; More did not introduce this sort of thing into the disputes of the day, but he displayed more of it than most and at no time troubled himself about such things as scholarly caution, chivalrous moderation, or (as his treatment of the Hunne case shows) even elementary truthfulness.

Moreover, these excesses seem to reflect traits not often remarked upon. Centuries of adulation have accustomed us to regard his treatment of Dame Alice as affectionate, and so, up to a point, it was. But it was also mildly contemptuous, and he did not scruple to print tales about women which everybody knew were aimed at her. He did not disguise his conviction that his second wife was a bit of a fool. The manner in which he singled out his daughters as examples of female intelligence cannot have been anything but galling to their stepmother, especially when his opinion of her was not expressed only by implication. Yet, in truth, every time that we learn of an argument between them, it seems to me that she had sense and unselfishness on her side. Or take the stories of More's wit, More the jester. In this it is certainly hard to separate truth from invention, and much may well have been ascribed to him that he never said. Yet what his early biographers reported of him was, presumably, what they thought was his and wished people to believe of one they admired—and some of the tales are disconcerting. The well-known story of the cutpurse and the justice, More's comment on a bad book turned from prose to verse ("now it hath at least some rime, no reason"), his

remarks about small women, and the lesson he taught
Ann Cresacre when he thought her too fond of jewels, all
have in common a rather unpleasing superiority to the
weaknesses of lesser mortals and a touch of hard severity.[88]
Perhaps none of these are authentic, though it is hard
to see why the last (and worst) should not be, but it
should be remembered that More's jests annoyed his
contemporaries, as Hall testified.[89] Witty persons make
enemies, and not without reason. There is one odd touch
about Sir Thomas's wit: a preference for the rather
crude in the "merry tales" with which he tried to leaven
the lump of controversy.[90] On two hardly apposite occasions, his similes reveal a preoccupation with virginity
and defloration which is a little strange and recalls his
insistence (in *Utopia*) that young men and women must
inspect one another naked before venturing on marriage.
When he rebuked the three bishops who tried to persuade
him to attend Anne Boleyn's coronation More was right,
but by what twist did the story of Sejanus' daughter (to
be deflowered so that her virginity should not stand in the
way of her execution for a capital offense) jump to his
mind?[91] It does not really make the point he was after.
And why, in explaining his failure to dedicate *Utopia*
to Wolsey, should he have described Peter Giles's action
in getting the work published at Louvain as a ravishing
of the book's maidenhead?[92] I am not, I hope, being
prissy: I am trying to get at the More inside the plaster
statue. The point is that his humor ran readily upon
such themes, and only those who tend to equate the
early sixteenth century with Rabelais would suppose that
in this he was typical rather than exceptional.

There is no question here of writing Sir Thomas down.
It is so difficult to see past the image erected by familial
and devotional piety that every scrap of evidence needs
to be carefully considered. And I wish to suggest that the

More of the 1520s, More the councillor, was a man aware of his powers, anxious to put them to practical use, capable of vanity and not always able to conceal his justified sense of intellectual superiority, ready enough to ride opponents down. To so outstanding a mind—possibly a poor politician but unquestionably capable of first-class statesmanship—the decade must have been most frustrating. He had office, he had profit, he had the ear and friendship of the king, and his ambitions did sufficiently tend that way to make such things not disagreeable. People respected his standing and envied him Henry's favor. But that he saw through the hollowness of friendship without influence, we know; nor would he forget Erasmus' severe regret that he was lost to letters. On top of this came his growing obsession with the dangers to the church and the faith which was forcing him to defend an institution that in his younger days he had been ready enough to criticize. And through it all he saw Wolsey pursue policies of war and empty grandeur which went counter to everything he believed in, while aware that the public and his friends were bound to associate him with these distasteful proceedings just because he seemed so much more influential than he was. Surely, More was throughout in a very false position, and he may well have re-read Hythloday's warnings against service to princes with a deepening regret derived from growing experience.

Yet in the end one more chance offered, all of a sudden. It, too, was flawed. Wolsey's fall, which led to More's elevation, arose from events in which More took his stand against the king's desires. Wolsey was removed not because he had failed in the sense in which More thought he had failed, but because he had not succeeded in the one thing that More did not want to see successfully accomplished. Once again his position was false. He owed the chancellorship to no previous power in Council but rather, ironically, his very lack of power: the king simply did not associate him with the fallen regime. No one seems ever to have commented on the very odd scene at the beginning of his tenure of office when the Duke of Norfolk, by special command, publicly presented him with much commendation as worthy of his new station.[93] This was so far from being common form that I know of no other single instance; clearly More's appointment was thought to be surprising, and the new chancellor needed introducing to a public barely aware of him. Henry thought of him as a skilful diplomat, an agreeable companion, a competent secretary, and possibly as a wise councillor whose instincts had now proven accurate. Above all, he clearly respected his abilities and regarded him as a friend, so much so that he was willing, for the time being, to let him contract out of the whole business of the divorce. No doubt he hoped in course of time to bring his obstinate friend round, but chiefly he, who prided himself on his knowledge of men, wanted this great man in high office. As he often did, he misjudged his man; himself so passionately convinced of the rightness of the divorce, he had lost the capacity to see that others might as firmly in conscience regard it as wrong. And he appears to have forgotten that part of More's charm for him was the very fact that he had never played the politician.

More, no doubt, accepted the great seal in part because it was difficult to resist Henry's pressure, but there is more to it than that. It is hagiography, not history or biography, to suppose that he must have been totally immune to the sensation of satisfied ambition which elevation of this kind would call forth in most people. More to the point, the offer came really as the culmination of the career on which he had entered—less reluctantly than is commonly thought—some twelve years earlier. To have

refused now would not only have offended one who
claimed to be a friend but would surely also have
stultified that dozen years. If he had endured so long in
the teeth of all the frustration and regret which the
Wolsey regime imposed on him, was he to retire at the
very moment when the years of waiting seemed about to
pay off after all, when power and influence were suddenly
and unexpectedly offered? Or, to put it another way, what
right had he to consider his private comfort and the
probability of a very difficult time when issues existed
(the king's marriage, the future of the church, heresy) on
which he felt strongly and in which he must at least
attempt to avert disaster? How disastrous the outcome
would be for him personally he could not have fully
foreseen; for one thing, he had a promise that the pressure
of the last two years to underwrite the king's proceedings
would not continue, and for another, the lengths to
which Henry was capable of going when he found himself
opposed by one whom he had honored with his friendship had not so far become apparent.

More explained his reasons for taking office in the
speech with which he opened the Parliament of 1529.[94]
He has often offended his partisans by the tone he used
about Wolsey, the "great wether" who had led the king's
flock astray, though in fact he was only following through,
in the rhetorician's fashion, a metaphor on which he had
embarked when he used the hackneyed description of
King Henry as shepherd of his people. The essential point
in his speech came at the start when he announced a
reform program. He declared the existing laws insufficient and out of date, and he alluded to the human
frailty which had produced "new enormities . . . among-
est the people" for which laws did not yet exist. Though we
must remember that we have only Hall's summary of
the speech, it is quite clear that reform of the realm was

foremost in the chancellor's mind, and from his mouth these were more than platitudes. The author of *Utopia,* the enemy of heretics who had witnessed Wolsey's negligent failure to arrest the decline of the church, had arrived at a point where he might think himself able to carry some of his ideas into practice. His answer to Hythloday might yet be justified. After all, one of the burgesses who listened to him from beyond the bar of the House was before very long to use the position of Henry's chief minister to reform state and church and reconstruct the commonwealth.

More, as we know, never got his chance. The humanist in power was to be as frustrated by events as the humanist working his way up had been by the cardinal's monopoly of power. In a way, of course, it was no fault of his that he so regularly found himself out of step and in a false position. The time was, for him, as thoroughly out of joint as it was convenient to Thomas Cromwell. Nor was More ever the conventional scholar unable to understand the reality of politics and power. He never made Reginald Pole's mistake of supposing that book-learning enables a man to teach the princes of this world their business. Indeed, if the analysis here put forward is anything like correct, More was not at all the scholar foolishly venturing into affairs. He was the trained common lawyer— possessed, that is, of a usual training for public life— with the ambitions and experiences of his kind and his station in life, fully aware (as his business letters to Wolsey show) what public service meant. If we knew nothing of *Utopia* or Erasmus, we should think More perfectly well placed in the company of such men as Dr. William Knight or Sir Brian Tuke. He was a thoroughly competent civil servant and councillor: let there be no mistake about this. But he was trying to serve at a time when his fundamental ideas stood in opposition to the fundamental desires of those in power. We may well prefer the *pax christiana* to the effects of Wolsey's foreign policy. In the struggle between the chancellor's conscience and the king's we may well award the palm to the first. But none of this alters the falsity of More's situation. The king's good servant throughout made the mistake of supposing that Henry wanted the service he was anxious to give, and not the service which would suit the king's very different purpose. In the last analysis, Hythloday was right.

NOTES

1. Allen, 3:356 f.; *LP*, 2:4438.

2. *LP*, 2: 3976, 4110.

3. J. H. Hexter, *More's Utopia: the Biography of an Idea* (Princeton, 1952), 133 f. I disagree, however, with his Appendix A, which denies that More could have been in Henry's service very much earlier than this.

4. Rogers, nos. 10, 14, 42 (p. 94).

5. Hexter, pp. 131 f.

6. Allen, 2:196: "Quamquam mihi revertenti pensio annua ab Rege decreta est, eaque plane, seu quis honorem spectet seu fructum, neutiquam contemnenda."

7. P[ublic] R[ecord] O[ffice], C 82/463. The common statement that the annuity was wholly charged on the petty custom is wrong (e.g., E. M. G. Routh, *Sir Thomas More and his Friends 1477–1535* [Oxford, 1934], pp. 92 f.).

8. In 1521–22 More was paid only £50 (PRO, E 407/67[3]), but this was made up by a cash payment of £150 for the following year (PRO, E 405/193). Thereafter payments reverted to half cash, half assignment, though in 1525 the assignment itself was divided between the petty custom and the parliamentary subsidy (PRO, E 405/195).

9. Allen, 4:20, 294.

10. Roper, pp. 11–12.

11. Rogers, no. 57.

12. Cf. Chambers, p. 175.

13. Allen, 4:506.

14. Huntington Library, El. 2655. More attended on October 29, 1518, October 27 and November 21, 1519, January 30, 1521, and May 15, 1526.

15. *LP*, 4:3926.

16. *LP*, 2:4125.

17. *LP*, 5:1610, referring to a bond of November 16, 1519.

18. Roper, p. 11.

19. PRO, Req. 2:2/76, 7/53.

20. *LP*, 2:4025, 4055; 3:491, 577

21. Rogers, no. 57.

22. Routh, *op. cit.*, p. 107.

23. Allen, 4:576.

24. Ibid. An unduly suspicious mind might suggest that Erasmus must have had his exaggerated information from More himself.

25. More's first Declaration belongs to 1521–22, as was to be expected (PRO, E 407/67/[3]). *Deputy Keeper's Reports*, 2: App. ii, 196–97, errs in assigning this to the following year. It is a draft book which shows that the sections of the Declaration were supplied by sub-departments before being copied fair into the final version.

26. *LP*, 3:3563 (November 26, 1523).

27. *LP*, 4:345, 1254, 1526; Rogers, p. 249.

28. Allen, 4:506, 576.

29. E.g., *LP*, 4: p. 870.

30. The date of the patent under the duchy seal (PRO, DL 28/6/23, which recites the document).

31. R. Somerville, *History of the Duchy of Lancaster* (London, 1953), p. 393. The date there given of More's appointment is out by a day.

32. All this is based on the Duchy accounts for More's time: PRO, DL 28/6/23–5. That for 1525–26 is missing.

33. Cf. Chambers, *Thomas More*, pp. 200 f.

34. *LP*, 4:2972.

35. *LP*, 3:1775, a warrant of November 18, 1521 to pay him a backlog of £80 arising out of two embassies abroad.

36. *LP*, 3:2239.

37. *LP*, 3:2900; 4:314, 2817.

38. *LP*, 4:2248.

39. Westminster Abbey Muniments, Miscellany, Treasurer's Accounts, MSS 23021, 23023 (1520–22). I owe this information to Dr. D. J. Guth.

40. *LP*, 4:3619.

41. Ely Diocesan Records, Register West G/1/7, fol. 43. I owe this reference to Mrs. Felicity Heal.

42. *LP*, 4:2527, 3380.

43. *LP*, 4:2972.

44. *State Papers of Henry VIII* (1830–52) [hereafter cited as *St. P.*], 1:124.

45. *St. P.*, 1:127.

46. *LP*, 2:3371, 3634, 3639, 3743, 3750, 3772, App. 38.

47. *LP*, 2:3976.

48. *Hanserecesse von 1477–1530*, D. Schäfer, ed. (Leipzig, 1905—),
Docs. 332, 448, 452. The negotiations filled the days July 19–August 12,
1520 and September 12–November 30, 1521; the commission for the
second phase was dated July 22, 1521. Since this paper was written,
J. M. Headley, in his introduction to *CW* 5, has noted the importance
of this record for the history of Sir Thomas More.

49. Ibid., Doc. 448, para. 55.

50. Ibid., Doc. 332, para. 33.

51. Roper, pp. 19–20.

52. *LP*, 4:1525, 1470.

53. *LP*, 4:1600(3), 1601. He was preceded not only by the two arch-
bishops, two dukes, a marquess, and a bishop, but also by two professional politicians in Sir Henry Guildford and Sir William Fitzwilliam.

54. *LP*, 4:3080, 3138, 3216, 3337.

55. *LP*, 4:5732, 5744.

56. Roper, pp. 36–37.

57. *LP*, 4:2638, p. 1399.

58. As early as 1518, Giustiniani commented on More's reputation
for justice (*LP*, 2:3976).

59. The only time that More was described as "secretary" was
during the Calais negotiations of 1520, when the Hanseatic envoys
called him 'secretarius regius' (*Hanserecesse*, 7:580). The official record
of the final agreement called him only "armiger," and the secretary
of Danzig even at this time knew that Pace was secretary: to him
More was, significantly, "comes [i.e., sheriff?] et civis Londinensis" (ibid.,
Docs. 336, 348). His promotion to the undertreasurership did not go
unnoticed when the two sides met twelve months later (ibid., Doc. 448,
para. 7).

60. *LP*, 2: App. 51.

61. *LP*, 3:76.

62. Rogers, nos. 77–79.

63. *St. P.*, 1:20.

64. *LP*, 3:1675, 1709, 1774 (October 1521).

65. Rogers, no. 109.

66. Ibid., no. 110.

67. Ibid., no. 117.

68. *LP*, 3:2636.

69. *LP*, 4:828.

70. *LP*, 3:2317.

71. *LP*, 4:2526.

72. *St. P.*, 1:176.

73. Ibid., 178.

74. Ibid., 181 f.

75. *LP*, 4:1083, 1154, 1237.

76. *LP*, 4:2397.

77. *Household Ordinances* (Society of Antiquaries, 1792), p. 160.

78. Allen, 3:286.

79. Rogers, no. 104.

80. Ibid., no. 105.

81. *LP*, 4:4562, 4604.

82. T. Stapleton, *The Life and Illustrious Martyrdom of Sir Thomas More*, trans. P. E. Hallett (London, 1928), pp. 136 f.

83. J. J. Scarisbrick, *Henry VIII* (London, 1968), p. 112; Rogers, no. 199 (p. 498).

84. Chambers, *Thomas More*, pp. 186 f., 254.

85. *Hanserecesse*, 9:402 f. The episode is discussed, not very satisfactorily, by M. E. Kronenberg, "A printed letter of the London Hanse Merchants, 3 March 1526," *Publications of the Oxford Bibliog. Soc.*, New Series, I (1947): 25–32. For the investigation see *LP*, 4:1962.

86. Routh, *Sir Thomas More*, p. 101.

87. For More's controversial writings cf. Rainer Pineas, *Thomas More and Tudor Polemics* (Bloomington, Indiana, 1968).

88. Ro. Ba., *The Lyfe of Syr Thomas More, Sometymes Chancellor of England*, ed. E. V. Hitchcock and P. E. Hallett (London, 1950), pp. 107 f., 129.

89. Edward Hall, *Chronicle* (London, 1809 ed.), p. 817: "it semed to them that best knew him, that he thought nothing to be wel spoken except he had ministered some mocke in the communicacion."

90. Pineas, pp. 92 f.

91. Roper, pp. 57–59.

92. Rogers, no. 32.

93. Roper, p. 39.

94. Hall, *Chronicle*, p. 764.

GERMAIN MARC'HADOUR

Thomas More's
Spirituality

The title of this paper calls for a word of explanation. The term "spirituality" itself needs some defining. It does not designate More's personal saintliness. A beautiful picture of his Christian personality emerges from all good More biographies, but my present object is more austere: it deals with More's principles, with the maxims that underlie his conduct, or at least express his ideals.

A man's spirituality is something wider than either his faith or his theology. More's *faith* is not perceptibly different from that of Erasmus; it is not hugely different even from Luther's. Countless Christians in his day shifted from the Catholic to one or another Protestant "confession" without a clear sense of the basic difference. A *theology* has greater complexity than a faith: it involves a certain systematizing carried along philosophical lines, it incorporates a *zeitgeist,* it can even reflect a temperament. Thus the *theologia positiva* championed by More tends to put curbs on deduction and speculation, on logic and metaphysics, while it advocates an ever fuller grasp of the sources through the tools of philology.

Spirituality is at the junction of theology and anthropology. It is conditioned by the believer's cultural, social, and even physical circumstances. In an original author, it is apt to be highly personal and even idiosyncratic. There is but one catholic faith. There are only a few schools of catholic theology. But scores, if not hundreds, of spiritual families, or sub-families, have flourished in the church. Some have become extinct because they were too closely linked with the mentality, the drives, the sensitivity, the secular values of their age. Others have undergone mutations so drastic that their old labels no longer really fit. Now this diversification reaches down to individuals. More as a spiritual author differs, not only from Thomas à Kempis or from Martin Luther, but also from his friends, Colet, Fisher and Erasmus; partly, perhaps, because he was a slightly younger man, and certainly because he was a lawyer, a layman, the father of a family, etc. More's spirituality was, of course, no more proof against change than were his physical features. The challenge of Luther was bound to modify its emphases. This consideration alone would justify limiting this assessment to the period before More was hit and shaken by the writings of the German Augustinian.

The title also says "Thomas More"—not "Saint Thomas," the canonized martyr who had shed his blood for the faith; not even "Sir Thomas," the good servant on whom knighthood was bestowed in 1521. This investigation will not go beyond the year 1520.

Three reasons seem to me to dictate this chronological limit: 1. Yesterday Professor Martz took us to "the very quick of More's spiritual being" by quoting generously from those late writings, which contain the ripest expression of More's Christian wisdom. 2. I myself have drawn primarily on those later works in various studies of More's spirituality.[1] By sheer force of quality and quantity, his post-Lutheran works loom large in those articles. 3. A certain thematic completeness has been achieved by E. E. Reynolds in his anthology, *The Heart of Saint Thomas*

More, as well as in my *The Bible in the Works of Saint Thomas More.*[2] No further documentation on such a vast field is needed now, but rather an attempt to reach some major joints and sinews of More's early spirituality.

Drawing the line at 1520 means excluding the main part of More's literary output, and perhaps as much as nine-tenths of his spiritual writings. Even his unfinished meditation on *The Four Last Things* will be left out, since its first editors date it about the year 1522, when More was forty-five and had already begun his cooperation with Henry VIII in refuting Luther's *Babylonica.*

The documents that remain to be examined after this drastic elimination are still numerous and manifold:

The Life of John Picus

More's *Pico* is an elaborate piece of work; because it was published at least twice in More's lifetime, and because it is openly devotional, it is of paramount importance to this study. The author, still in his twenties, dedicates it to no ordinary friend, but to a cloistered nun, "his right entirely beloved sister in Christ," Joyeuse Leigh, whom he greets "in Our Lord." Despite the title, what mattered most to More was the anthology from Pico's *Opera:* to these "works" [3] the biography serves as an introduction. More enjoys greater freedom for self-expression in the excerpts than in the *vita:* he chooses which pieces to include, expanding or contracting, or even paraphrasing his model. The works, in fact, represent the larger part of the volume.

Already an expert dietician of the soul, More serves a balanced meal to his spiritual guest. The proportion of Old and New Testament citations is strikingly parallel to that in More's overall output,[4] and here too the Book of Psalms predominates, for a whole psalm (Ps. 15) is commented on verse by verse.[5] Did More read Pico's *Opera* before he read Erasmus' *Enchiridion,* which came out in early 1503? Pico's

letters to his nephew John-Francis breathe a militant spirit
not unlike that of Erasmus' christian knight, and his twelve
"weapons of the spiritual battle" provide a similar military
metaphor. Pico inculcates the necessity of unremitting labor,
of not grudging the price, of entering through the strait gate
(Matt. 7:13), and of "leaving the dead alone with their
dead" (Matt. 8:22). Christ's soldier fights intrepidly, not
fearing "them that slay the body" (Matt. 10:28). Tremble
only if thou livest in sin, for then "the devils shall take thy
soul from thee" (Lk. 12:20). These devils are More's addition to Luke and to Pico's letter: in his later quotations of
this verse More will use the vaguer subject *they*. The devil,
however, is by no means absent from Pico's works; for
example, in the sixth rule of his spiritual battle he conjures
up that perpetual and mighty foe, "like a wood lion . . .
seeking whom he may devour." [6] Another source of temptation is the world: being more eager to please God than
man (Acts 5:29), a true Christian annoys his fellowmen,
not only the pagans among them but also the tepid Christians, so he must brace himself for some form of persecution. Besides, he is his own persecutor, since the flesh is
constantly rebelling against the spirit (Gal. 5:17).

The universal remedy for these evils, the source of all
comfort, the peerless model, is Christ—Christ crucified;
More, after Pico, details the suffering of the Saviour, the
scourging, the nails and the spear, the blood and the water
flowing from his side.[7] Perhaps at More's suggestion, a
woodcut of the crucifix adorns the title page of the earliest
known edition of his *Pico,* complete with all the instruments of the Passion and a kneeling adorer. Of greater
significance than the nature of His sufferings is the spirit
of obedience with which Christ embraced the human condition to fulfil His Father's merciful plan: He was "obedi-
ent even unto the death" (Phil. 2:6–8). In Christ obedience,
which can be a servant's attitude, becomes that of a son.
We are "God's servants by nature, children by his grace,"

hence twice bound to do His will. How dare we shrink
from what Our Lord accepted? "The servant is not above
his master" (Matt. 10:24): if Christ went to heaven through
hardships, we must not look to go there on featherbeds.[8]
The reward in store for us there is out of proportion with
our labors here below. God will welcome us as His
"blessed children": More adds the word *children* in translating the *benedicti* of Matt. 25:34, by which the supreme
Judge invites the just into His bliss.[9] Pico's "A Prayer to
God" closes and climaxes the selection. In his rendering of
it More puts greater stress on God's fatherhood than his
model does. Pico's last hexameter

Non Dominum, sed te sentiat esse Patrem

is expanded by More into three lines, the last correspond-
ing to one word: *Patrem.*

He may thee find, o well of indulgence,
In thy lordship, not as a lord, but rather
As a very tender-loving father.

Both say *"AMEN"* after that, and rightly so; to grasp the
mystery of God's fatherhood is the ultimate of the Gospel.
"All our reward" says another last line, is that "we may
behold God and Jesus-Christ." [10] This beholding is the
fruit of love rather than knowledge; true love, the fruit of
Christ's spirit abiding in us, makes us friends to God, and
"ghostly friends" to each other as More explains to Dame
Joyeuse in his first paragraph. Prayer is the breathing of
that inner life. It is spontaneous, as it were, and yet it
should be practised also as an exercise. How? First of all
by reading the bible. I must, after many others, quote
Pico's capital advice to his nephew and spiritual heir:

Thou mayst do nothing more pleasant to God, nothing
more profitable to thyself, than if thine hand cease
not day nor night to turn and read the volumes of Holy
Scripture. There lieth privily in them a certain heavenly

strength, quick and effectual, which with a marvellous power transformeth and changeth the reader's mind into the love of God.[11]

Clearly, from first page to last, the Pico volume is a spiritual nosegay, specifically Christian, resolutely geared toward the increase in "godliness" of both compiler and reader. If the flowers have artistic fragrance too, because they were culled from a Florentine garden, Pico's appeal lies not in his being "the phoenix of geniuses," but in his having through bitter experience understood the vanity of all things earthly, and made up his mind to forsake the world and follow Christ.

More's Early Verse

More's Latin poems,[12] written for the most part in his youth, are of a different character. Few have to do with the life of the spirit. Three *epigrammata* conjure up a New Testament scene—the Banquet of Herod with, for its gory dessert, the head of John the Baptist. Three others rail at the absurd corollaries drawn by worldly clerics from trite Pauline maxims: "Knowledge puffeth up" (I Cor. 8:1); "The letter killeth" (2 Cor. 3:6); "Where the spirit is, there is freedom" (2 Cor. 3:17).

More the poet is a common sense moralist, of the Horace or La Fontaine type, or rather, to name his explicit model, of the Lucian type: *Castigat ridendo mores*. But can a sharp line be drawn between merely ethical and properly spiritual edification? Can "virtue" be divorced from the practice of God's commandments or even the imitation of Christ when the whole context of reader and author is christendom? To tell us that More was a saint, Roper calls him "a mirror of virtue": virtue in the sixteenth century carried essential religious overtones.[13]

One theme especially is cherished by philosophers and saints alike: the meditation of death. It is central to More's youthful asceticism. All the seeds that will grow and spread their branches in page after page of *The Four Last Things* and *A Dialogue of Comfort* have begun to sprout vigorously in the early poems. Die we shall certainly (epig. 37); though we cannot tell when, we know it will be soon (epig. 55); nay, we are in the process of dying all the time, even now while we talk (epig. 57). This pondering on the brevity and brittleness, the tenuity and the very nothingness (epig. 112) of man's estate here below breeds a healthy, a realistic "contempt of this life" (epig. 51).

The death in 1503 of Queen Elizabeth, Henry VII's wife, provided More with a perfect "ensaumple" to illustrate his *memento mori*. He is too much of a gentleman and too fine an artist to turn every line of the *Rueful Lamentation* into a sermon. The main point, however, the most universal in its application, the most chastening and searching, is made right from the start:

> O ye that put your trust and confidence
> In worldly joy and frail prosperity,
> That so live here as ye should never hence,
> *Remember death* and look here upon me:
> Ensample I think there may no better be.

Elizabeth is a Christian queen, not a philosopher. Death in her eyes is God's "mighty messenger" (line 19); she prays (lines 12, 18, 40, 65, 67), and seeks prayers (lines 63, 77), and her last words, especially, are pure prayer:

> . . . Thy infinite mercy
> Shew to thy servant, for lo now here I lie.

Thy servant: this so motherly and affectionate creature never calls God "father"; admittedly the liturgy of the

dead also emphasizes the lordship of the creator and task-
master while appealing to His mercy. Was More's intense
devotion to the fatherhood of God only virtual and dor-
mant until Pico aroused and catalyzed it, or until he himself experienced what it means to be a father? More's first
child Margaret—for whom he was to coin the epithet
"daughterly"—may well have been born before her father
tackled Pico's elaborate metrical prayer.

One of More's many approvals of the monastic life occurs in stanza XI of the elegy, where the queen, addressing
her sister Bridget, congratulates her on having forsaken the
world of her own free choice, before the world forsook
her:

> Lo here the end of worldly vanity.
> Now well are ye, that earthly folly flee
> And heavenly thingès love and magnify.
> Farewell and pray for me, for lo now here I lie. (ll. 74–77)

The passage from life to death is the most drastic of
mortal changes. Remembering it leads inevitably to reflections on mutability, on the unpredictable turns of our
destiny:

> O mortal folk, that we be very blind!
> That we least fear, full oft it is most nigh. (ll. 54–55)

("Very blind," of course, means "truly blind," as "very
father" at the end of the versified prayer means "true,
authentic father.") No need to point out how closely the
Book of Fortune, and More's advice to those who trust
fortune, and also his captions to the pageants representing
the cycle of man's life from the cradle to the grave and
beyond, age after age into eternity, show him haunted by
the transiency of the sublunar stage, and eager to awaken
from their perilous sleep those who are tempted to make it
their dwelling city. Since God alone abides and can reward

us with everlasting life, let him be the sole center of our desires.

In permansuro ponite vota Deo

is the last line of the last stanza, the final lesson of the fact, abundantly ascertained and documented, that we are all puppets in a vast pageant. No priest is needed to draw the lesson, a poet does it quietly, "sitting in a chair." [14]

As for the blindness of man in the face of his future, More will pause—and point out that he cannot refrain from pausing—to wonder at it in the *History of Richard III*, when he paints Hastings elated by his luck at the very time he is being drawn into the jaws of his devourer.[15]

Man's inability to control his fate and to achieve permanence led various philosophers to advocate apathy, whether gloomy or serene. More's defunct queen, functioning now as a Christian preacher, exhorts her family to take everything in good part:

Take all a worth, for it will be none other (l. 59).

When reason has done its part and discredited fortune-seeking, faith takes over and points out that, since a good and wise God is the shaper of man's destiny, He should be trusted to make every turn of fortune a good turn if it is well taken. Even the *Merry Jest* of the sergeant who played the friar expresses that confidence:

God may turn all,
And so He shall,
I trust, unto the best.[16]

God expects, of course, man's cooperation. Charity, which is the bond of perfection, can bind only willing souls. God's failure to gain entrance into His creature's will, having made it free, is as it were mirrored in the fruitless attempts of More's Edward IV to glue together the inner circle of his kinsmen and allies: the ties of blood and the grace of sacramental matrimony having proved too weak for this, he urges them to remember an even nobler fealty, the "proper badge given by Christ to his soldiers." [17] If they cannot agree and unite for charity's sake, they are no longer the knights of Christ, they no longer fight under his banner.

This is one of several "sermons" in *Richard III;* but even the light pieces More and Erasmus translated from the Greek of Lucian were not, in their eyes, without a spiritual "utility." [18] Their model was an atheist, granted, but then they are not borrowing his theology, they are catching and echoing the healthy laughter by which he tries to shame us out of our native gullibility and our fondness for lying, "our itch for telling tall stories and our readiness to believe them." Lucian is also a dispenser of "truth and good sense in everything," a deflater of pretence and pomposity, a professor of sanity and balance. Nor is he useful only to the worst fools among us. Augustine would have profited from reading him, and Chrysostom quotes him at length in his *Homilies on the Gospel of John:*

> for, while he advocates the Cynics' way of life, austere and content with little (unfastidious), he thereby indicts the soft, nerveless (emasculated) ways of such as pamper themselves, and thus extols the moderation and the frugal simplicity of Christian life, in a word that strait and narrow path that leads to life.[19]

What Is Truth?

The recurrence of the problem of truth and lying in More's works across the years shows that it was frequently, if not constantly, in his mind. We shall see how he practically solves it and how he notifies the republic of letters about his solution.

That itch for fiction and exaggeration works especial havoc in our devotion to the saints, More writes in the letter dedicating his *Lucian* to Ruthal: the spice of legend in their biographies is an affront to Christ, "who is the truth, and who wanted his religion to stand in the naked truth." [20] This protest of More's, first published in 1506, had gone through at least five editions by 1520. It was his best-known original composition. Thus the world was prepared to see him champion the truth for the sake of the truth, long before he was forced to defend it with his blood.

In nuda veritate: the Christian Revelation, to deserve its name, is an unveiling, a laying bare of all that man needs to know about God and God's ways with men. But not all truths are thus naked. Some are sheathed, as it were, in teguments of human flesh. Some sore truths beg to be dressed in bandages of mercy. Because its recipient is a vessel of clay, truth often calls for cautious handling. We must keep this in mind when we open More's letters to his friends. His first extant letter to Erasmus, of early 1516, is carefully penned; More, who is now putting the final touches to his *Utopia,* knows that whatever he writes will probably find its way into print. This particular letter was actually in print within a few months. Now listen to its opening lines:

> Since our last encounter, Erasmus darling, I have heard from you three times. If I claimed to have also written you thrice, even were my lie supported by a solemn oath, you might refuse to believe it: you of all men know full well that I am lazy at writing letters, and that I am not so scrupulously truthful as to consider a fib as abominable a crime as the murdering of father and mother.[21]

The rest of the letter precisely illustrates More's tampering with the truth through a mixture of obliging silence and diplomatic shifting. While in Flanders in the summer of 1515, he had discussed with Erasmus and with Wolsey's representative, Richard Sampson, the likelihood and the wisdom of a canonry in the cathedral of Tournay being conferred on the Dutch humanist. The offer was not a fat one, nor was it without its strings, compulsory residence being the most galling. Erasmus was reluctant to accept it. Meanwhile the benefit was rumored to have gone to some-one else:

> At this news, I concealed what I had understood, namely that you were not much interested, and I per-suaded Mountjoy and Sampson to write Wolsey that the benefit had already been granted to you, and that, as the matter stood at this stage, a change was impossible unless some more advantageous provision were first made for you.[22]

Mountjoy, who was holding the city on behalf of Henry VIII, and Sampson, who was taking possession of the diocese on behalf of the cardinal, had first-hand knowledge of Erasmus' reluctance to become a canon there, and yet they seem to have connived with More's stratagem. The trick worked; Wolsey did promise to offer Erasmus some-thing better: "so he owes you that fatter sinecure," [23] More would later say. The real untruth, the black lie, lay in the cardinal's failure to keep his pledge. More's conscience in the affair is so clear that he takes the chance of his con-fession being read by all Europe, including Wolsey, the chief victim of his "dissimulation," and this at a time when he himself was, Ammonio tells Erasmus, a regular and an early caller upon the mighty cardinal.[24]

Yet in the same letter, More reports that he has dis-suaded Maruffo from dissembling in the exchange nego-tiations he was carrying on in Erasmus' behalf. More's reason was that the subterfuge, designed to dodge the nuisance of Chancery redtape, was not needful.[25] We learn

from a later letter (June 1516) that Maruffo did actually
recur to some innocent strategy in his dealings with Archbishop Warham over the transfer across the Channel of
Erasmus' English money. The client's letter to Warham
did not tally with his agent's statement, which was bound
to arouse a suspicion of dishonesty in the archbishop's
mind. More took upon himself to repair the blunder by
some explanation of his own, so as to convince Warham
that both men were trustworthy: "Now if your next letter
to the archbishop," More writes to Erasmus, "discredits
this fiction of mine, I'll have to look round for yet another
invention, or else I shall ruin his Lordship's confidence in
me while I'm trying to restore his trust in another person." [26] More's conduct, which obviously gives him no
qualms, bears a certain kinship to the situation ethics so
much in the fore today. Men of a sterner fiber would
shudder at such elasticity just as Raphael Hythlodaeus
frowned at intellectuals who were ready to put up with the
compromise and flattery that inevitably attend—and in his
eyes defile—diplomatic and political involvement. More's
plea to Hythlodaeus, advocating a "more civil, more flexible philosophy," [27] is paralleled in his letter to Erasmus
of October 31, 1516—the *Utopia* was in the press—by a
remark concerning Latimer. When asked to take in hand
John Fisher's initiation into the Greek language, Latimer
said he had made different plans and would not alter them.
"You know," writes More, "how to philosophers of this
type their own decisions are as binding as immutable laws,
such is their cult of constancy." [28]

Evidently the two humanists, of London and Rotterdam,
have agreed to disagree with such petrified postures as Latimer's and to be ready for change should circumstances rec-
ommend it. They prize affection above admiration. Sincerity in friendship can justify a measure of pretence, just
as it can dictate a change in plans. If the end does not by

itself alone justify the means, surely the doer's intention
imparts to the deed its moral and spiritual coloration.
Total impartiality, like absolute constancy, is apt to be
inhuman. As justice driven to extremes become injustice,
truth-telling, when it is over-rigid, can reach *rigor mortis*
and lose the plasticity of life. Of course to More truth
possesses an objective solidity; it transcends the human
person; it exists even when unsuspected or ignored or
denied. Yet a spiritual truth has a personal dimension too.
Its existential complexity is never fully grasped; it is
monstrously disfigured by those who simplify it by divorc-
ing it from its context.

More needs no advocate, since no sensible person would
impeach his behavior in the dealings we have heard him
report upon. Most people, however, might expect higher
scruples from a martyr for the truth. Perhaps one could
say that More, by loading the scales in favor of Erasmus,
was not only being a true and trusty friend, but was also
being true to the common good, true to England and
christendom, that he was righting an old wrong, or re-
ducing the harm done to Erasmus by the cardinal's neglect.
In the second instance, Erasmus and Maruffo had made arrangements that were awkward, but not dishonest. More's
concocted explanation dispelled or prevented all suspicion
of foul dealing. The complete tale would have taken more
time to tell than those concerned could spare to listen. The
essential truth was safe, namely that the surface discrep-
ancies between the two statements were not a sign of sinis-
ter intent.

One is reminded of Kingsley (in the line of Latimer
and the "philosophers of that type," in the tradition of
Augustine himself, against Jerome) accusing Newman of
championing untruth, because Newman had underlined
the actual limits—psychological, or pedagogical—of truth-
telling. The problem is perennial. I encountered it again

last month in the bush of Guyane, when a doctor asked me: "Should this expectant mother be told that she's being treated for leprosy?" A parallel analysis of mercy-lying and mercy-killing might help to reach practical conclusions toward both: the latter is legal in Utopia, and More, we have seen, feels no guilt when indulging in the former.

Another parallel is suggested by More's conduct in the Tower. He is awaiting death for his fidelity to an old order as well as to the old faith. He has been a champion of law and order as a Christian, he has enforced them as a magistrate; yet he is constantly trespassing against prison regulations, with St. John Fisher as his accomplice, when they exchange letters and small presents: both obviously feel sure that this neither offends God nor can harm any man. More no doubt approved his family's resorting to bribery in order to circumvent iniquitously hard bylaws: he, the *candidissimus,* would never condone anything that was black, but such breaches of the letter of the law, like his breaches of the literal truth, were better than white, they were splendid. It is not impossible, moreover, that, great joker as he was, he enjoyed a certain amount of mystification in actual life, as he enjoyed a good measure of it in literature. A complete examination of this delicate problem should take into account the basic irrationality of real men, which Erasmus asserts so eloquently, under More's aegis, in *Moriae Encomium.* The truth these men worship is a vigorous entity to be grasped notionally and spiritually, but it is also a vital identity to be achieved gradually with "a holy ambition," a message to be conveyed both faithfully and charitably— *veritatem facientes in caritate* (Eph. 4:15).

Letter to a Certain Monk [29]

Some folly is welcome, as an ingredient of a full humanity. Too much of it is perilous, and some forms (the

maniac) are criminal. As early as 1506, prefacing his Lucian
translations, More had shown the charlatans preying on
the gullibility of the crowds. He denounced this and similar dangers again in his 1519 "letter to a certain monk," at
which I invite you to take a good long look before you
examine the rest of his correspondence. The monk, whose
name More charitably omits—he was probably John Batmanson the Carthusian—had written to warn him against
the subtle venom of Erasmus. More attention has been
paid, so far, by most of us, to the 1515 Letter to Martin
van Dorp, which may be superior as literature, and
broader in scope; but the answer to the monk has far
greater relevance to my present purpose. It is an essay in
spirituality, More's longest and most elaborate. Dorp was
a professor, and More's discussion with him bears on things
of the mind, on academic programs and methods. But a
monk is essentially a "ghostly" person; his *contemptus
mundi,* More holds, should extend to all secular pursuits,
including, besides literary gossip, an undue appetite for
knowledge, and an excessive interest in speculation. More
calls his unnamed correspondent "frater in Christo caris-
sime," that is "right entirely beloved brother in Christ,"
the same form of address he used for Sister Joyeuse Leigh.
The letter's importance is increased by the fact that it was
printed three times in the summer of 1520, twice at Antwerp, once in Basel. No other writing of More, except of
course its companion pieces, the letters to Lee, went through
so many editions in such a brief period.

It is very much a humanist manifesto, and to superfi-
cial readers it has sounded anti-monastic. No one who has
wrestled with it line after line can come away with that
feeling. There is no tinge of irony in the sentences pro-
claiming More's love of the monastic institution: "Nowhere," he asserts, "is there a good man who does not
cherish and hold dear all religious orders." [30] The burden

of More's indictment is: let the monks remember their
vows, let them be true to the spirit of their state, by putting
first things first, by never sacrificing what is essential to
what is subsidiary or peripheral. Excessive concern with
gesture, with ritual, is, of course, the standard complaint:
More here echoes the Erasmian slogan. This is not, he remarks, a specifically monastic abuse, but a propensity of
popular religion in all climes and all ages; it is, however,
a worse disgrace in religious orders, whose members are
expected to show greater refinement, more practical awareness of the Gospel beatitudes, and to avoid the grosser and
cruder aberrations.

More's chief, and characteristic, onslaught is against the
spirit of private ownership, which prefers the personal to
the communal in all fields. This spirit, he says, has crept
back into the cloister, whence it was assumed to have been
ousted once and for all by the community system. Monks
will show an unholy attachment to the details which dif-
ferentiate them from the laity, or among themselves. Thus
certain practices, limited to an order, end up looking more
important than God's commandments. Corporate pride,
corporate possessiveness, rise upon the ruins of self-con-
tempt and complete renunciation of one's goods. The
monk shows concern, not only for his order's holiness, but
for its image. After listing various symptoms of this centrif-
ugal and disruptive tendency, More comes to a very broad
statement, not easy to translate, but often quoted nonetheless for the light it throws on the *Utopia* and perhaps
because it is felt to throw a most searching light into
More's soul, to reveal one of the foundations if not *the*
foundation of his spirituality:

It was a major provision of God's wisdom that he instituted all things on a community basis. Christ in his turn
was highly provident when he endeavored to restore the

spirit of community after mankind had set up private ownership. He saw all too well that, given the corruption of his nature, man's undue love of his private interests never fails to harm the common good.[31]

This sweeping statement is all the bolder as it ascribes to Christ's personal teaching what is practiced by the early Christians.[32] More lists manifold expressions of fallen man's irrepressible possessiveness: my purse, my plot of land, my craft or corporation, my patron saint, my private devotions. At least twenty times in this letter he uses the words *privatum* and *proprium* and their opposites *commune, publicum,* and even *vulgare.*

There is a healthy partiality. Friendship, extolled by all Christian humanists, implies predilection. The basic piety which accepts and fosters personal ties shines bright in Thomas More: he loves his home, his *alma mater* Oxford, his city, his country, his king. More's insistence on common as against private ties and tasks and interests is prompted by the monstrous hypertrophy in early Tudor England of the sense of private property—leading to the cruel and disproportionate repression of theft.[33] More may have felt inclined himself to grow passionately attached to the persons and things around him—jealous of London's privileges, jealous of England's independence. The tone of his retort to Brixius betrays a love of his motherland for which he apologizes to Erasmus, begging the courteous readers not to raise him too high while he treads the earth still, and to condone his all-too-human sentiments, including bouts of passion.[34]

One manifestation of the public spirit is the assumption of civic responsibilities. How is More, then, going to defend Erasmus, that resolute and successful dodger of involvement? He portrays him, in the fulfilment of his personal vocation, as a hero of dedication to the common cause, whose work benefits the whole church, indeed the whole world. Erasmus is like a sun in the sky of Europe, shining even for the ungrateful users of his lights. He sacrifices himself to the common good: though rewards have eventually fallen into his lap, his studies were financially unrewarding, and they were detrimental to his health: so he cannot be suspected of selfish motives.[35]

What is most common is in a way the finest and rarest: sun and stars outshine all man-made jewels.[36] God's commandments, and the theological virtues, which are common and "plebeian"—as are "humility and the fear of God"—constitute an ideal so high that nothing can be added to it: it is a dangerous illusion to fancy that you fly above that level! [37] The commoner More—he was a half-hearted "lord" for two and a half years—loves all that is held in common: things, opinions, the language, and that universal flair called *sensus communis*. He would like logic to be as plain and common as walking or eating bread, and logicians to use everybody's words in their current meaning.[38] One might add that More's spiritual doctrine is one of commonplaces: the "two spurs, the one of fear, the other of love," which "spur forth thine horse through the short way of this momentary life to the reward of eternal felicity" [39] are devotional clichés, as are Fisher's "two millstones," the nether of fear, the upper of hope, which grind man into perfect flour for God's sacrificial cakes.[40] What are these spurs, borrowed, through Pico, from an immemorial tradition? Not feelings only, but *things,* events to be pondered:

> Never forget these two things: that both the Son of God died for thee, and that thou shalt also thyself die shortly.[41]

Thus wrote the Piedmontese earl before he was thirty to a youth of his day, and More, then a coming man in his

twenties, picked this text up, out of hundreds, to translate
it and to offer it to a young nun from his neighborhood.
No wonder then if a woodcut of the Crucifixion meets the
reader's eye before he opens *The Life of John Picus*. In his
short span of life that amazingly studious philosopher had
read all the books, yet the only text he cared to scrutinize
on his deathbed was a crucifix, "that he might ere he gave
up the ghost receive his full draught of love and compas-
sion in the beholding of that pitiful figure." [42] Images, the
author of *The Image of Love* had argued, "be but laymen's books," not needed by "religious men and folk of
more perfect life." But, answers More, "they be good books
both for laymen and for the learned too." [43] God's love
for mankind is written nowhere in letters so big and glow-
ing as on a carved or painted cross with the Word of God
nailed to it. The crib of Bethlehem and the other scenes
of Christ's infancy are absent from More's writings; if this
does not mean they were altogether absent from his life,
since his love of the liturgy is well substantiated, it shows
at least how fully he shares the "theology of the cross," to
use a phrase which has been applied to Luther's teaching
but which befits the fifteenth century hardly less than the
sixteenth. Calvary is ubiquitous in Pico's letters of spiritual
direction, and in his maxims. *Stat crux dum volvitur orbis:*
this motto of the Carthusian Order, which More never
quotes but by which he learned to live, vividly envisions
the cross of Christ as the axis of the universe, the fixed
shaft around which our mortal destinies revolve, moved by
a loving gravitation, though to our hazy eyes the spinning
seems to be caused by the kicks of goddess Fortune's heel.
The Renaissance, in preference to this cosmic simile, likes
to gaze on divine Love as mirrored in the features of the
Man of Sorrows: iconography here also corroborates the
trends perceptible in literature. The vernacle—the image

of Jesus as stamped on Veronica's veil—adorns one of the finest borders in the Basel *Utopia* of 1518.

We have already met the other spur, the fear of death, as a leitmotiv in More's early poetry. He was, however, anxious to exorcise that fear: you all remember his page in *Utopia* about longing to die and be with God—a theme that was to recur frequently in his prison writings.[44]

The contemplation of Christ crucified, Pico says, classically since St. Paul himself had said it in other words, is love's richest fuel. More endorses this message by selecting it for translation. Yet to the monk he writes that Erasmus, by his studies, gathers more merit, and is a greater benefactor of the church, than are the religious through their prayer. A rather unexpected scale of values! Where is the medieval *lege minus, ora magis?* Where is Pico's sighing admission to his friend Poliziano that the weary circuitous approach to God through knowledge is disappointing even where it succeeds, since the heart, not the intellect, truly grasps and possesses its object? [45] Where is Colet's recent reflection to Erasmus, that all those books, of which there is no end, never really lead us to the purification, the illumination, the union with God, which are our sole aim, and the short cuts to which are love and imitation of Jesus? [46] Is More then, in the fervor of his apology for Erasmus the professional student, repudiating entirely the mystical element, the dark unknowing urge for God which his spiritual director imbibed so deeply from his Neoplatonic masters? Allowance must be made for the *ad hominem* bias of this particular letter. The prayer More minimizes is not the soul's uplift toward God "in spirit and in truth," but the recitation of prayers: these are apt to become a mere routine and at the worst they become a hideous caricature of prayer. To drive his point home, More recounts two anecdotes instancing monstrous deviations in the cult of

Our Lady, and he also inveighs vehemently against certain silly ditties in honor of the saints.[47] His thrusts at false devotion are the satirist's own way of defending true devotion.

If one were to label More's piety on the basis of the above observations, Carthusian would not do, despite More's admiration for and huge debt to the Charterhouse.[48] Franciscan seems to me to be least inadequate. Grey friars, More points out, lead that mixed life of action and contemplation which Christ's apostles also led.[49] Whether or not Stapleton is well-informed when he tells us that More, as a young man, considered joining the Order of Friars Minor,[50] More himself tells us that he holds no Order in higher esteem; he also expressly indicates that the *Utopia* was colored, or rather discolored, by the drabness of voluntary poverty as practiced by the sons of St. Francis.[51] The ideal of common ownership, however lofty and arduous, held an enormous and practical appeal for the Assisi Poverello, who, his first biographer tells us, "wanted all things to be common to all men," and managed to enlist tens of thousands of people from all classes into his classless, moneyless army, or rather family. The same dream clearly haunts More's mind: how could it be otherwise since he believed that, until it came true, God's initial and presumably perennial plan for mankind and Christ's restorative program remained unfulfilled? Let the leaven of the Gospel be as active as the leaven of self-love—*philautia,* Folly's progeny—Christians will irresistibly be led to share everything as true brothers, and the radiance of their carefree happiness will inevitably exert a fascination on the rest of mankind, and thus heal the foulest sores brought about by covetousness.

Even Fortune, it seems, owes her bane and blight chiefly to her favoritism, which goes counter to God's impartial providence:

And at adventure down her giftes fall:
Catch whoso may, she throweth great and small,
Not to all men, as cometh sun or dew,
But, for the most part, all among a few.[52]

Akin to communism and to commonplace is communion,
a theme central to More's spirituality. A keen sense of
human solidarity, the vision of the commonwealth as one
family, with citizens but no subjects, with a ruler but no
"prelate," only a father, underlies his passion for the
church as "one corporation mystical . . . communion of
men together with God . . . society of all good folk in
the mystical body of Christ." [53] He labors to reactivate,
revivify the metaphor of "the body politic," of the sovereign
as "head," of the people as "members." He even says in an
epigram that the whole kingdom is but one man.[54]

Vice, like virtue, assumes many forms, yet all vices, all
evils, have one ultimate origin: "our common foe—*hostem
illum communem,*" the wily serpent, God's universal op-
posite, "the secret source from which practically all sins
flow as from a polluted spring," [55] the chief upsetter of
God's merciful design. Death we need not fear, but him we
should certainly fear, though not to the point of being
paralyzed: he is a cunning illusionist, and a wicked alche-
mist, capable of transfiguring himself into an angel of light,
and of turning our good to evil, just as God turns our evil
to good.[56]

More's Correspondence with Erasmus

A high proportion of More's extant letters before 1520
are known to us only through scraps incorporated by
Stapleton in his *Thomae Mori Vita,* so we cannot even tell
whether they were written in English or in Latin. His
correspondence with Erasmus, although some of it was

"doctored" before publication, might well, as a sequence, provide the truest index of More's daily preoccupations; these letters bring us the ring of his voice as a speaker. One cannot but be struck by their secular tone, as if the layman had pledged to himself never to dispense pieties to one who was the acknowledged proponent of *pietas*. There was no lack but rather a surfeit of pious phraseology around them, even in diplomatic dispatches and peace treaties. More won't be a preacher. Nor has he much patience with fellow-humanists, even priests, like Dorp or Brixius, when they sound as if they were in a pulpit.[57] Preaching is a sacred function, totally different in More's eyes from teaching, even from theological teaching. The debating divine in his letter to Dorp is ridiculous rather than dangerous; he is an academic crank. So is the Oxford don who leads the onslaught against Greek studies: More's rebuke, however, is not prompted by this preposterous hostility on the part of a divine against the best theology and the New Testament itself, but by the blasphemous impiety with which he dares to conduct the war from the pulpit during the holy season of Lent.[58] A similar profanation arouses More's anger at the Coventry friar he describes in his letter to Batmanson.[59] Such fellows are spiritual evildoers. Quibbling questionists are also dangerous when they choose moral casuistry for their sporting ground; their hair-splitting is bound to foster that dodging of the Gospel absolutes, that minimalism which in the seventeenth century was to draw the sarcasms of another fervent layman, Blaise Pascal.[60] Your casuists teach men "how close they can come to sin without sinning," a sorry contrast with the uncalculating spirit of the Sermon of the Mount, with the "large manner" illustrated by Zacchaeus the publican.[61]

More's reserve in his letters to priests—who were the majority of his penfriends—may have been inspired also by

a keen sense of the majesty of God, whose name should
not be lightly used, whose written word especially should
be handled with the utmost reverence. "O Holy God of
dreadful majesty", this first line of Pico's prayer is not
belied by the last line, addressing God as "a very tender-
loving father." God's "state is kingly" to More, as it would
be to Milton.

Unlike his more formal epistles to the university of
Oxford and to Gonell, his children's tutor, which are
explicitly religious in tone and content, More's letters to
Erasmus, I had begun to say, are strikingly secular. The
classics are frequently quoted or alluded to, the Bible is
not. Scripture appears as a topic, not as an influence, still
less as an all-pervading atmosphere. More's friendship with
Erasmus is a matter of Castor and Pollux, not of David
and Jonathan. The immortality he refers to has little to
do with the fervent hope which makes his conversation
glow when he talks of heaven with his friends; [62] instead it
is the literary fame, which, he feels, is guaranteed him
through Erasmus' writings.[63] "Fate," "destiny," the "powers
above" are mentioned, Christ is not. More's letter of June
1516 is almost amusingly financial, coming as it does from
the author of *Utopia* in the last stage of his pregnancy with
Utopia: "I lack time to achieve stylistic elegance, and indeed to think," More writes, "but let's forget about law-
suits and literature, let's talk of money first, since that
comes foremost: *de pecunia primum, utpote re primaria.*" [64]
He is being jocular here, but money matters will again fill
his four extant letters to Erasmus of September and October of that Utopian year, demonstrating, in his own words,
that he is "by no means a paltry handler of other people's
money." [65] Modesty, toleration, freedom from vainglorious
leanings—attitudes that are not specifically Christian—
loom large in this correspondence. So do the commonplaces
about the fickleness of fortune, the vicissitudes and un-

predictability of everything earthly: "Dawn shattered my dream, but real kingdoms do not last much longer"; [66] Peter Giles is having a bout of tribulation, but not everyday is a *noverca*,[67] and Peter is sure to enjoy better times; Ammonio has died of the sweating sickness, but "what fate brings we must accept." [68] Knowing More from other sources, we feel certain that each of these events turned him toward God as the only solid good, as the center of permanence, as the provident dispenser of tribulation and comfort. No doubt he would pray in his heart, and also orally with the liturgy, that "amid all the changes of this world, our hearts may settle firmly where true joy is to be found"; [69] but, addressing Erasmus, he appears shy of any expression that might sound even remotely like a sermon. The spring of 1520, however, brings a startling change of tone. More has perhaps just interviewed Edward Lee, and the harshness of Erasmus toward the young Englishman may have appeared unchristian to him. He sounds gently rebuking:

> The peace settlement between you and Lee is constantly being broken, and neither will plead guilty. I won't adjudicate in your quarrel, I can only lodge a plea for mutual pardon . . . You need not be warned, or exhorted to such modesty as befits a true christian, since in all the drudgery this affair has inflicted on you, Christ has been your sole aim. He alone, then, should be now before your eyes. His reward for your labors will be the more solid since this ungrateful world does not care to repay you, nor could it even though it felt grateful.[70]

Gentleness Versus Holiness?

A common misrepresentation of More is to see him exclusively as *suavissimus, mellitissimus,* the gently smil-

ing charmer that he could actually be. His spiritual code
has likewise been labeled as *bonhomie,* heaven's path
made engaging and attractive, and, again, there is truth in
this too. In *The Four Last Things* especially, one of his
themes is that "virtue bringeth his pleasure and vice is not
without pain": he quotes a string of Old Testament verses
to support his contention.[71] The most impressive authority
for this view is Christ Himself saying: "My yoke is sweet,
and my burden light," [72] and cursing the scribes and phar-
isees because they have made God's law unbearably hard.
Early reformers often likened the commandments of the
Roman church to the pharisaic ordinances, and emphasized the ease and lightness of the Gospel. When the young
messenger of the 1529 *Dialogue* uses this cliché, More
shows some impatience, launching into a highly significant
parenthesis:

> What ease also call you this, that we be bounden to
> abide all sorrow and shameful death and all martyrdom
> upon pain of perpetual damnation for the profession of
> our faith? Trow ye that these easy words of his easy
> yoke and light burden were not as well spoken to his
> apostles as to you, and yet what ease called he them to?
> Called he not them to watching, fasting, praying,
> preaching, walking, hunger, thirst, cold and heat, beat-
> ing, scourging, prisonment, painful and shameful death?
> The ease of his yoke standeth not in bodily ease, nor
> the lightness of his burden standeth not in the slackness
> of any bodily pain (except we be so wanton, that where
> himself had not heaven without pain, we look to come
> thither with play) but it standeth in the sweetness of
> hope, whereby we feel in our pain a pleasant taste of
> heaven.[73]

When he thus summarizes what one might call "the
spirituality of the Cross," More is not striking a new note.

He had expatiated on the jealousy of God, a quarter of a
century earlier, following Pico's list of the properties of a
true lover.

> The first point is to love but one alone . . .
> [God will] in love no parting fellows have . . .
> Part will He none, but either all or nought.[74]

The terms are as stark and simple, as totalitarian and ex-
clusive, as anything written by St. John of the Cross, the
mystical exponent of *Todo y Nada.*

NOTES

1. See in particular, *"Obediens usque ad mortem:* a key to St.
Thomas More," *Spiritual Life* 7 (1961): 205–22; "Le symbolisme de la
colombe et du serpent," *Moreana* 1 (Sept. 1963): 47–63; "How a
Christian Lives in an Affluent Society," *Franciscan Herald and Forum
42,* no. 11 (Nov. 1964): 332–40; "Saint Thomas More," in *Pre-Reforma-
tion Spirituality,* ed. James Walsh (London, 1965), pp. 224–39; "For
the Winning of Christ," *Westminster Cathedral Chronicle, 69* no. 5
(May 1965), 84–86.
2. E. E. Reynolds, *The Heart of Thomas More: Readings for every
day of the year* (London, 1966); Germain Marc'hadour, *The Bible in
the Works of Thomas More,* 5 vols. (Nieuwkoop, B. De Graaf,
1969–); hereafter cited as *The Bible.* For a synoptic view of this in-
ventory, see my *Thomas More et la Bible* (Paris, 1969), passim.
3. Three times in the dedicatory letter More refers to the selection
as being the essence of his volume: "These works, more profitable
than large, were made in Latin by one John Picus . . . The works are
such . . . Which works I would require you gladly to receive . . ."
(Rogers, p. 10; in this paper all quotations from Rogers and the 1557
English Works [*EW*] are given in modern spelling).
4. Roughly one third Old Testament, one third Gospels, one third
Epistles.
5. It will be remembered that Erasmus too began his paraphrastic
undertakings in 1515 with a Psalm.
6. *EW,* p. 22. This image, from 1 Peter 5:8, will remain a favorite
with More throughout his life. It occurs repeatedly in his Tower
writings.
7. The main references are Matt. 27:26, 34, 38 and John 19:34,
which will be found in vol. II of my *The Bible.*

8. These terms summarize Pico, but they come from More's advice to his children as recorded by Roper right at the beginning of his *Life of More*.

9. "Come, ye, my blessed" for "venite, benedicti" would probably have sounded awkward even in Tudor English, so that stylistic considerations dictated the use of some noun. For the *maledicti* of Matt. 25:41, More uses *people* to support the participle. *Children* is an addition to which he also recurs in 1 Cor. 4:15.

10. John 17:3. This comes at the end of the "interpretation upon this psalm *Conserva me*" (*EW*, p. 20); it also ends the prose section of the volume.

11. *EW*, p. 13.

12. All quotations are from *The Latin Epigrams of Sir Thomas More*, ed. L. Bradner and C. A. Lynch, Chicago 1953. When I give the scriptural reference instead of the number of the poem in the 1953 edition, it is because the reader will find parallel quotations in *The Bible*.

13. The Erasmian phrase *pietas literata*, a possible definition of Christian humanism, is matched in More's English by "virtue and learning," which occurs in his *Pico* (*EW*, p. 1), as well as in Roper's *Life* (p. 7): More's children were "in virtue and learning brought up; whom he would often exhort to take virtue and learning for their meat, and play for their sauce."

To temper the epigram *Scientia inflat* (no. 244) one might quote More's canonization of *pietas literata*: "Cunning much edifieth and profiteth joined with charity" (see *The Bible* under 1 Cor. 8:1).

14. *Epigrams*, Appendix II, pp. 117 and 238. More, by designing the pageants and then by captioning them, mobilizes two forms of art for purposes of edification: he preaches sermons in painted cloth, as the mediaeval churches had preached in stained glass or frescoed walls.

15. *The History of Richard III*, ed. R. S. Sylvester, *CW* 2: 52/13: "O good God, the blindness of our mortal nature! When he most feared, he was in good surety; when he reckoned himself surest, he lost his life."

16. See the reference and other, more complete formulations in *The Bible* under Rom. 8:28.

17. "charitatis symbolum suis militibus dedit"; see *The Bible* under John 13:35.

18. "voluptatemque cum utilitate conjunxerit," Rogers, p. 11/2.

19. "dum aspera parvoque contenta Cynicorum vita defenditur, mollis atque enervata delicatorum hominum luxuria reprehenditur. Necnon eadem opera, Christianae vitae simplicitas, temperantia, frugalitas, denique arcta illa atque angusta via, quae ducit ad vitam, laudatur" (ibid., p. 12/29).

20. "Nec veriti sunt eam religionem contaminare figmentis, quam ipsa Veritas instituit, et in nuda voluit veritate consistere" (ibid.,

p. 13/65). On truth's innate vigor, see *Utopia*, *CW 4:* 200/169, and Rogers, p. 169/132. See also "inflexibilem veritatis regulam" in Rogers, p. 60/1138.

21. "praesertim quum ipse me tam probe noscas, et ad scribendas epistolas pigrum, neque tam superstitiose veracem ut mendaciolum usquequaque velut parricidium abominer" (Allen, 2: ep. 388; cf. *SL,* p. 65).

22. "Dissimulato quod intellexi, beneficium animo non admodum respondere tuo, suasi ut rescriberent tibi esse concessum, remque in eo esse statu ut mutari non possit nisi tibi de meliore fortuna prius esset provisum" (Allen, ibid.; cf. *SL,* p. 67). The first word of the sentence rings a highly Morean bell—the indictment of that "deep dissimuler," the Duke of Gloucester (*Richard III, CW 2:* 8): "Ah! Whom shall a man trust?" (ibid., p. 83).

23. "et pinguius tibi debere" (ibid.). In September (Allen, 2: ep. 461), More was still hoping that Wolsey would "eventually match with real things his superlative words in praise of Erasmus: ut verba illa tam egregia aliquando rebus exaequet."

24. "Nemo temperius eo matutinum Eboracensi portat ave" (Allen, 2: ep. 389).

25. "Non est, inquam, hac simulatione opus" (Allen, 2: ep. 388).

26. "Quod si hoc quoque commentum meum tua revincat epistola, jam dispiciendum est mihi aliud quippiam, ne meae apud dominum fidei jacturam faciam, dum alterius laboro resarcire" (Allen, 2: ep. 424).

27. *Utopia*, ed. E. Surtz and J. H. Hexter, *CW 4:* 99. The book is so well known, and should be reread so constantly, that I leave it for the reader to draw further parallels, with the help of the *Index:* e.g. under "Stoicism," "Epicureanism," "Lesbian rule," "equality of sins," etc. More's "indirect approach" (p. 99) bears the same wise and innocent affinity to the politics of expediency as his acceptance of inconsequential lies, prompted by something like "legitimate defence," bears to criminal mendacity.

28. "Scis huiusmodi philosophis quam immutabiles leges sunt sua decreta—credo quod delectentur constantia." I disagree here with Allen's correction (2: ep. 481): Erasmus' emendation must have been *sunt,* not *siue* and there is no need to add *faciant; quod* before the subjunctive obviously means "because," not "that."

The same concern for appearing consistent is responsible, in Erasmus' eyes, for the continued hostility of a Louvain theologian: "murmurat nescio quid, gloriae causa, ut ne parum vir constans videatur" (Allen, 2: ep. 584, addressed to More on May 30, 1517). Both Erasmus and More would be remembering the ridicule poured by Dame Folly on the paradoxes of some Christian moralists who out-Stoic the Stoics in their lack of nuances, saying for instance: "Let the whole universe perish rather than tell a single lie, however light and slight" (*Moria*, Section LIII: "*Potius . . . universus orbis pereat . . . quam unicum quantumlibet leve mendaciolum dicere*").

Latimer's fossilism appears also in his Ciceronianism. He objects to words like *sabbatum* in Erasmus' version of the New Testament: "nullum prorsus verbum admittit quod Romanis auribus fuerit insolens" (Allen, 2: ep. 481).

Erasmus' contemporaries were less critical than we tend to be toward the skill he employs at accommodating himself to his correspondents: *chameleonta agere* was no pejorative phrase, versatility was no disgrace. Erasmus' 1504 letter to Desmarais, justifying the flattery he had used in his *Panegyric* of Philip, is worth re-reading: Paul too, he says, uses pious adulation, "laudans ut emendet . . . Certe Plato, certe Stoici mendacium officiosum permittunt sapienti." (Allen, 1: ep. 180).

29. Rogers, pp. 165–206. *SL* gives the second half in English, pp. 114–43. For a French translation of the whole letter, see *Moreana*, no. 27–28 (November 1970). All references here are to the text as in Rogers.

30. "Haud dubito neminem esse virum usquam bonum cui non religiosorum ordines omnes eximie chari cordique sint" (ll. 1093).

31. "Multum providit Deus cum omnia institueret communia; multum Christus, cum in commune conatus est rursus a privato revocare mortales. Sensit nimirum corruptam mortalitatis nostrae naturam non sine communitatis damno deamare privatum" (ll. 1136 f.; cf. *SL*, p. 129). The prefix in *deamare* suggests wanton, uncontrolled attachment.

32. See *Utopia, CW 4*: 218/5 and commentary on it at p. 519. The reference to the Jerusalem community is even clearer in the *Supplication of Souls;* see *The Bible*, under Acts 2:45 and 4:32 f.

33. See the denunciation of this punishment in *Utopia, CW 4*: 71 f. et passim.

34. "Dum adhuc inter mortales versor, nondum plane relatus in divos (ut in re ridicula rideamus), non verebor, inquam, quin aliquid et in me condonaturus sit humanus lector humanis—quos hominum nemo prorsus excussit—affectibus" (Allen, 4: ep. 1096). The repetition of *homo/humanus* resembles the same repetition in the 1499 *disputatiuncula*, when Erasmus calls upon Colet to give a human interpretation to the human words uttered by the Son of Man in His agony.

35. Rogers, p. 201/1370 f., especially line 1377: "Ecclesiae toti profuit"; line 1379: "totus orbis"; line 1400: "publicum omnium commodum"; line 1404: "non absque publico studiorum fructu."

36. *Utopia, CW 4*: 157/13.

37. Rogers, p. 196/1162 f.: "cum omni prorsus populo christiano communia, cujusmodi sunt virtutes istae plebeiae—fides, spes, charitas, Dei timor, humilitas, atque id genus aliae." Cf. lines 1118, 1165, 1169, for God's commandments, and such lines as 1472: "in communibus istis christianismi virtutibus."

38. To Dorp, Rogers, p. 40/428 f., climaxing at line 432: "communis nimirum sermo est . . ." Speech being the mirror and the shaper of

thought, these crazy logicians are also naturally miles "a communi hominum sensu" (l. 621).

39. Pico's letter to his nephew, *EW*, p. 13.

40. *The English Works of John Fisher*, ed. J. E. B. Mayor (London, 1935), p. 114: "Saint Gregory compareth hope and dread unto two millstones wherewith meal is made."

41. *EW*, p. 13: These lines are part of the last sentence of Pico's "first epistle to his nephew John-Francis," of 1492.

42. *Pico*, in *EW*, p. 8.

43. *Dialogue concerning Heresies*, in the page added in 1531 to book I, ch. 2; in *EW*, the objection, voiced by the messenger, is on p. 114, and More's answer on p. 117.

44. See my *Thomas More et la Bible*, p. 199 f.: "Désir d'être avec le Christ."

45. Gianfrancesco Pico, whose *Vita Pici* More is here translating, quotes from his uncle's *De Ente et Uno*, dedicated to Poliziano. More's English (*EW*, p. 7) is not very felicitous; the original reads: "Sed vide, mi Angele, quae nos insania teneat: amare Deum dum sumus in corpore plus possumus quam vel eloqui, vel cognoscere; amando plus nobis proficimus, minus laboramus, illi magis obsequimur; malumus tamen semper per cognitionem numquam invenire quod quaerimus quam amando possidere id quod non amando frustra etiam inveniretur" (p. 20 in the 1498 Venice ed. of Pico's *Opera*).

46. Letter of June 1517 (Allen, 2: ep. 593): "Erasme, librorum et scientiae non est finis . . . Meo judicio nulla alia via assequemur quam ardenti amore et imitatione Jesu."

47. Rogers, pp. 197/1197 f., for the two stories; pp. 188/850 f., for More's angry reference to the "orationes rhythmicae." *SL*, p. 120: "This Folly contains less folly and even more true piety than do . . . certain hymns which some of your friends think place all the saints under their obligation."

48. The London Charterhouse, adjoining Lincoln's Inn, was an obvious choice for the period of probation More desired, quite apart from the high reputation of St. Bruno's order, which Moria herself reflects: "Carthusienses, apud quos solos sepulta latet pietas" (Section LX). But More never shows partiality to the Carthusians. Among the "blessed fathers" whom he envied when on May 4, 1535 he saw them "going to their deaths as bridegrooms to their marriage" was a Bridgettine, Richard Reynolds, as was also Richard Whitford, another good friend of More's. Pico, his first hero, died in the white cowl of the Dominicans. More was a great benefactor of the Canterbury Benedictines, who in gratitude granted him letters of fraternity.

49. Rogers, pp. 201/1355 f.

50. *Thomae Mori Vita*, ch. 2: "Minoritarum institutum arripere cogitabat."

51. Rogers, p. 201/1357: "Ordo Minoritarum, quo (nisi me fallit

opinio) nullus est ordo sanctior." In his December 1516 letter to Erasmus, he tells of his dream about being king elect of his beloved Nowhere and visiting his island "conspicuus paludamento franciscano" (Allen, 2: ep. 499). There is charming irony in *conspicuus*, since the gray uniform of undyed wool was calculated to make everyman, king included, "inconspicuous." See *SL*, p. 85.

I am planning a book on More's Franciscanism. Among the most characteristic features is "glad poverty," connected in the *Book of Fortune* with Bias, Democritus etc., but typically Franciscan too. Pico was under the influence of Savonarola the Dominican, but More's book on him goes by priority to a Minoress. There is far more privacy in a charterhouse than in a Franciscan friary, where you have no little house or plot of land for yourself; you live, as do the Utopians, "under the eyes of all" (*Utopia, CW 4*, 83). When a Carthusian smugly contrasts monastic stability with the ceaseless globe-trotting of that tourist, Erasmus, More rebukes him for canonizing sedentariness, "as if to reside forever in the same spot . . . were the last word in sanctity" (*SL*, p. 137).

52. Sig. ¶₆v in *EW*, the 7th stanza of "Thomas More to them that trust in fortune."

53. See *The Bible* under Eph. 5:23. More's purgatory in *The Supplication of Souls*, and his heaven, especially at the end of *A Dialogue of Comfort*, are essentially communities: one is a "socia exultatio," the other, a "socia expiatio." How antipodic to the legend of Renaissance individualism! Nor was More alone in having this sense of the group, and of man's social dimension. Even religious movements had stressed community rather than poverty or chastity in the fifteenth century; the most original foundation of the period was "the Brethren of the common life," who schooled both Erasmus and Luther.

54. *Epigrams*, no. 94: "Totum est unus homo regnum, idque cohaeret amore."

55. Rogers, pp. 194/1074 f. (*SL*, p. 127). *Callidus* is used of the devil in lines 860, 928, 1114 and 1294.

56. Rogers, pp. 195/1115 f.: "Deo omnibus in rebus oppositus."

57. To Dorp, Rogers, pp. 42/509 f.; to Brixius, ibid., p. 237/894: "ut fere concionantis quoque personam induas." Cf. Erasmus' letter to More of c. November 1520, claiming the right to occasional irreverence and irrelevance on the ground that his books are not "sacred," whereas preaching is a sacred function—the words *sacrae concioni* occur three times (Allen, 4: ep. 1162).

58. To the University of Oxford, Rogers, pp. 114/77 f.: "majestatem sacrosancti concionatoris officii . . . in ipso Dei templo, in altissimo pulpito."

59. Rogers, pp. 197/1221 f.

60. *Les Provinciales*, "sur le sujet de la morale et de la politique de ces Pères" (Cologne, 1657) were so harsh in tone that Pascal—as

More had for the *Responsio ad Lutherum*—used a pseudonym, Louis de Montalte.

61. For Zacchaeus, see *The Bible* under Luke 19:8.

62. "Cum amicis sic fabulatur de vita futuri saeculi ut agnoscas illum ex animo loqui, neque sine optima spe" (Erasmus to Hutten, Allen, 4: ep. 999). This portrait of More, published in 1519, is rather secular on the whole, but it seems that Erasmus had More in mind too when, dedicating to Abbot Paul Volz the new edition of his *Enchiridion,* in August 1518, he wrote: "There are monks who hardly belong to the outer circle [of Christians], while there are twice-married men whom Christ admits into the inner circle of his friends" (Allen, 3: ep. 858).

63. Allowance should be made, of course, for More's intention to be both classical in tone and flattering to Erasmus. There is no reason to think he was repudiating the lesson he had borrowed from Pico: "We should seek for the glory and praise, not that cometh of men, but that cometh of God" (*EW*, p. 12), a theme he had repeated in his letter to Gonell. Even earlier, when Lady Fame (sixth pageant) claims to "confound the power of death" by causing dead men to live "in perpetual memory," Time rebukes her empty boast.

64. Allen, 2: ep. 424, not published in Erasmus' lifetime. The scholastic adage, "Primum vivere, deinde philosophari," expresses much the same view.

65. "nequaquam malignum dispensatorem alienae pecuniae" (Allen, 2: ep. 468). Most of these letters are also in *SL*, pp. 65 f.; this one, p. 76.

66. "Hoc tamen me consolor, quod vera regna video non multo prolixiora" (Allen, 2: ep. 499).

67. "neque omnis dies noverca" (Allen, 2: ep. 601). The stepmother is ubiquitous in classic literature. See R. S. Sylvester's review of *L'Univers de Thomas More* in *Renaissance News* (1964), p. 322, citing J. L. Vives. After explaining to his children the first of Quintilian's declamations—"for the blindman against the stepmother," More sent a number of letters to the Spanish humanist, requesting him to compose a rejoinder defending the stepmother. This is no. 1 in Vives' 1521 *Declamationes*—"pro noverca contra caecum." More impressed Erasmus by his own affection toward the three successive stepmothers his father's repeated remarriages gave him: "Huic cum noverca . . ." See p. 68 of my *Thomas More vu par Erasme* (Angers, 1969). In *Apology,* ch. X (EETS, ed. A. I. Taft, p. 51), More speaks of the last one, still alive, as "my mother-in-law."

68. "Quod sors feret ferendum est" (Allen, 3: ep. 623).

69. "inter mundanas varietates" was a burden of the late Pierre Mesnard's song; it occurred both in his private letters and in more formal circulars to fellow-academics. See *Moreana,* 22:106 and 107; 23: 85. It comes from a collect for the fourth Sunday after Easter in the

Roman missal: "ut inter mundanas varietates ibi nostra fixa sint corda ubi vera sunt gaudia."

70. "Non es vel admonendus, opinor, vel hortandus, ut exhibeatur abs te vere christiana modestia, cujus labor in tota re uni desudat Christo, qui tibi solus ob oculos debet observari: a quo solidiorem tanto referes gratiam, quanto magis hic referre mundus neque ingratus curat neque gratus potest" (Allen, 4: ep. 1090). This sermon was published by Erasmus in *Epistolae ad diversos,* August 1521.

71. The "many plain texts of Holy Scripture" about buying hell with greater pains than are needed to buy heaven will be found in *EW,* p. 98.

72. See *The Bible* under Matt. 11:30.

73. *EW,* p. 143, which is book I, ch. 18 of the *Dialogue concerning Heresies.*

74. *EW,* p. 28, stanzas 1 and 2 of "the twelve conditions of a lover," developing the first condition.

LIST OF PARTICIPANTS

Name and Affiliation

ALDEN, JOHN J. W. Acadia University
ALKIRE, JENNIFER R. Yale University Press
ALLENTUCK, MARCIA City College of New York
ALWANG, JANET Glastonbury, Conn.
ANDEREGG, MICHAEL A. Yale University
AVILA, SISTER TERESA St. Joseph's College
BARONE, JULIA St. John's University Press
BEAN, J. M. W. Columbia University
BENINCASA, FREDERICK St. John's University
BLACKBURN, ELIZABETH Wisconsin State University
BLANCHARD, E. SHEILA North Illinois University
BOTTINO, REV. EDWARD St. John's University
BOULTON, JAMES University of Nottingham
BRAUN, ROBERT Farmingdale, N. Y.
BRENNAN, JOHN St. John's University
BRODWIN, LEONORA L. St. John's University
BUNCE, JAMES E. St. John's University
CADDEN, DAVID Polytechnic Institute
CAHILL, VERY REV. JOSEPH, C. M. St. John's University
CAROL, LOIS New York, N. Y.
CAROL, RAYMOND L. St. John's University
CARROLL, GERARD L. New York, N. Y.

CASE, ELISABETH Cambridge University Press
CAVALIERE, L. St. John's University
CAVANAUGH, REV. JOHN R. St. John Fisher College
CHUDOBA, BOHDAN Iona College
CLARK, MARION St. Thomas More Society
COHEN, RUTH STEINKRAUS Westport, Conn.
COOGAN, BRO. ROBERT, C. F. C. Iona College
COWHERD, R. G. Lehigh University
DEAKINS, ROGER LEE New York University
DE BALLA, BORISZ St. John's University
DENNEN, GERARD New York, N. Y.
DESMOND, REV. DONALD St. John's University
DEVINE, REV. RICHARD J., C. M. St. John's University
DICK, JOHN RUSSELL Yale University
DICKENS, A. G. Institute of Historical Research
DICKENS, MRS. A. G. Institute of Historical Research
DI LEONARDO, GARY Fordham University
DIRCKS, RICHARD J. St. John's University
DIRVIN, REV. JOSEPH I., C. M. St. John's University
DOUGAN, SARAH B. Cambridge University Press
DOYLE, DANIEL Williamsport Area Community College
EARL, D. W. L. University of New Brunswick
ECKSTEIN, LEON Seaford, N. Y.
ELTON, G. R. University of Cambridge
EMERY, RUTH Rutgers University
ESCHBACH, EDITH K. St. Thomas More Society
ESMONDE, MARGARET P. University of Miami
FAGAN, EDWARD T. St. John's University
FELL, SISTER MARIE LEONORE College of Mt. St. Vincent
FIDELER, PAUL Lesley College
FISHMAN, JOEL Bronx Community College
FITZGERALD, GERALD E. St. John's University
FITZGERALD, HONORIA Fordham University
FRANCOIS, MARTHA E. Northeastern University
FRECKER, HELENA Memorial University of Newfoundland

FUIDGE, NORAH Yale University
GALLARDO, ALEX St. John's University
GERTY, URSULA M. Greenlawn, N. Y.
GESNER, MARJORIE E. Michigan State University
GILLARD, WILLIAM St. John's University
GITMAN, JOSEPH United States Merchant Marine Academy
GRIFFIN, WILLIAM D. St. John's University
GRINDEL, REV. CARL W., C. M. St. John's University
GUTH, D. J. University of Michigan
HARDISON, O. B., JR. Folger Shakespeare Library
HARRIER, RICHARD New York University
HASTINGS, MARGARET Rutgers University
HAVIGHURST, ALFRED F. Amherst College
HEADLEY, JOHN M. University of North Carolina
HECHT, J. JEAN Columbia University
HILL, W. S. New York University
HILLERBRAND, HANS City University of New York
HOFFMAN, ROSS Fordham University
ISABEL, SISTER Immaculata College of Washington
JAMES, DAVID B. Yale University
JENSEN, KENNETH St. John's University
JONES, COLIN H. Cambridge University Press
KANE, JAMES F. Kane-McNeill Inc.
KEHOE, REV. RICHARD J., C. M. Northampton, Pa.
KENNEDY, VERONICA M. S. St. John's University
KENNEDY, W. H. J. New York, N. Y.
KONECSNI, JOHNEMERY Caldwell College
KOSS, STEPHEN E. Barnard College
KUTTNER, STEPHAN G. University of California
LABALME, MRS. GEORGE, JR. Barnard College
LAFFERTY, JOHN Caldwell College
LAKEY, DONALD E. University of Wisconsin
LAWLER, THOMAS M. C. College of the Holy Cross
LEHMBERG, STANFORD University of Minnesota
LE VENESS, FRANK PAUL St. John's University

LEVINE, JOSEPH M. Syracuse University
LEVINE, MORTIMER West Virginia University
LILLY, EDWARD P. Washington Technical Institute
LIPKING, JOANNA Bread Loaf School of English
LOOMIE, REV. ALBERT J., S. J. Fordham University
LYNCH, MARY St. John's University
LYONS, J. LEONARD Bridgeport, Conn.
MCDONALD, JUSTICE MILES Supreme Court of State of New York
MCCARTHY, JOSEPH F. X. Fordham University
MCGARRY, BRO. PATRICK S., F. S. C. Manhattan College
MCGILL, THOMAS F. J., JR. West Roxbury, Mass.
MCGRATH, L. W., JR. West Roxbury, Mass.
MACALUSO, PETER F. Montclair State College
MANDEVILLE, SISTER SCHOLASTICA St. Louis University
MANLEY, FRANK Emory University
MARC'HADOUR, REV. GERMAIN Université Catholique, Angers
MARIUS, RICHARD University of Tennessee
MARKLE, JAMES A. The Thomas More Society, Detroit Mich.
MARTIN, WILLIAM F., ESQ. Martin, Clearwater & Bell
MARTZ, LOUIS L. Yale University
MEERSE, PEGGY C. University of Illinois
METZNER, PATRICIA Windsor Locks, Conn.
MILLER, CLARENCE H. St. Louis University
MLADEN, LEO Long Island University
MONTE, BRUCE St. John's University
MULLER, DOROTHEA R. C. W. Post College
MURPHY, CLARE M. University of Rhode Island
MURPHY, JOHN J. St. John's University
NELSON, WILLIAM Columbia University
O'DONNELL, SISTER ANNE M. Trinity College
O'KELLY, BERNARD University of North Dakota
OLIN, JOHN C. Fordham University

OSBORN, JAMES M. Yale University

PAOLUCCI, ANNE St. John's University

PARKS, GEORGE B. Queens College

PEGNAM, REV. FRANCIS J. St. Thomas More Parish, Rochester, N. Y.

PELLEGRINI, R. St. John's University

PERPETUA, SISTER MARIE Immaculata College of Washington

PRALL, STUART E. Queens College

REINHARDT, RT. REV. MSGR. MARION J. St. John's University

RICE, EUGENE F., JR. Columbia University

RICHARDSON, W. C. Louisiana State University

ROONEY, MIRIAM THERESA Catholic University

RUSSELL, REV. RICHARD R. Yale University

RYAN, SISTER JOAN St. Joseph's Convent

ST. PETER, GEORGE M. Fond du Lac, Wisc.

SCHMITT, HERMAN M. St. John's University

SCHOECK, RICHARD J. University of Toronto

SCHWEITZER, PAUL Pelham, N. Y.

SHAPIRO, HAROLD I. Hofstra University

SIH, PAUL K. T. St. John's University

SILKE, REV. JOHN J. Manhattan College

SLAVIN, A. J. Folger Library

SOMERVILLE, ROBERT E. Columbia University

SORLEIN, ROBERT P. University of Rhode Island

SPENGLER, ANNE New York, N. Y.

STAFFORD, EUGENE F. Iona College

STAPLETON, ALFRED B., ESQ. Providence, R. I.

STRAUSS, FELIX Polytechnic Institute

SURTZ, REV. EDWARD, S. J. Loyola University of Chicago

SYLVESTER, RICHARD S. Yale University

SYMES, REV. JOSEPH, C. M. St. John's University

THOMPSON, CRAIG R. University of Pennsylvania

TINNELLY, REV. JOSEPH T., C. M. St. John's University

TRAINOR, VERY REV. JOHN J., C. M. St. John's University

TUCKER, MELVIN J.   State University of New York at Buffalo

VINCITORIO, GAETANO L.   St. John's University

WALKER, BENJAMIN H.   Allied Stores Corporation

WATKINS, DAVID R.   Brandeis University

WEBB, C. JENKINS   Boston College

WEMPLE, SUZANNE   Barnard College

WILLIAMS, IRVING J.   St. John's University

YOUNG, ARCHIBALD M.   University of Western Ontario

YOUNG, ROBERT J.   St. John's University

ZEEVELD, W. GORDON   University of Maryland

PROGRAM

Edward T. Fagan, *Moderator*
St. John's University, School of Law
10:30 A.M.
Richard J. Schoeck
University of Toronto
"Common Law and Canon Law
in Their Relation to Thomas More"
11:30 A.M.
Discussion
1:00 P.M.
Luncheon

FRIDAY AFTERNOON

O. B. Hardison, Jr., *Moderator*
Folger Shakespeare Library
2:30 P.M.
Louis L. Martz
Yale University
"Thomas More's Tower Works"
3:30 P.M.
Discussion
5:00 - 7:00 P.M.
Cocktails

SATURDAY MORNING, OCTOBER 10

James M. Osborn, *Moderator*
Yale University
10:30 A.M.
G. R. Elton
University of Cambridge
"Thomas More as Councillor (1517-1529)"
11:30 A.M.
Discussion

1:00 P.M.
Luncheon

SATURDAY AFTERNOON

Richard S. Sylvester, *Moderator*
Yale University
2:30 P.M.
Rev. Germain Marc'hadour
Université Catholique, Angers
"Thomas More's Spirituality"
3:30 P.M.
Discussion

COMMENTATORS

A. G. Dickens, *University of London*
Denys Hay, *University of Edinburgh*
Stephen G. Kuttner, *University of California*
Richard Marius, *University of Tennessee*
Clarence Miller, *St. Louis University*
Bernard O'Kelly, *University of North Dakota*
Craig R. Thompson, *University of Pennsylvania*
Rt. Rev. Msgr. Marion J. Reinhardt, *St. John's University, School of Law*

PROGRAM COMMITTEE

Richard S. Sylvester (Chairman), *Yale University*

Edward T. Fagan, *St. John's University, School of Law*
O. B. Hardison, Jr., *Folger Shakespeare Library*
James M. Osborn, *Yale University*
David R. Watkins, *Brandeis University*

ARRANGEMENTS COMMITTEE

Gaetano L. Vincitorio (Chairman), *St. John's University*

J. M. W. Bean, *Columbia University*
Richard J. Dircks, *St. John's University*
Ruth Emery, *Rutgers University*
William Gillard, *St. John's University*
J. Jean Hecht, *Columbia University*
John J. Murphy, *St. John's University, School of Law*
Stuart E. Prall, *Queens College*

INDEX

Adam, 65
Adrian VI, Pope, 105
à Kempis, Thomas, 126
Alington, Alice, 9, 63–64, 66–67
Allen, P. S., 119–20, 122, 154–59
Ammonius, Andreas, 136, 150
Anglo-American Conference
 (1965), 20
Antony (character in *Dialogue of Comfort*), 66, 78
Antwerp, 140
Archbishop of Canterbury. *See* Cranmer, Morton, Warham
Aretas, King, 77
Arundel, Earl of. *See* Fitzalan, Henry
Audley, Sir Thomas, 45–46, 63, 65

Bacon, Francis, 22
Barnes, Robert, 8
Basel, 140, 145
Bassett, Mary, 60, 78–79, 82
Bath, Bishop of. *See* Clerk
Batmanson, John, 140, 148
Baumer, F. L., 55
Baynard's Castle, 28
Benedictines, Order of (Canterbury), 156
Bethlehem, 144
Bias, 157
Blackfriars, 27–28
Bodin, Jean, 54

Boleyn, Anne, 10, 63, 80, 114
Bolt, Robert, 42
Bombasius, Paulus, 88
Boniface VIII, Pope, 49
Bradner, Leicester, 153
Bray, Sir Reginald, 97
Brentford, 107
Brian (Bryan), Sir Francis, 49, 99
Brian, Chief Justice Thomas, 17, 49
Bridge Street, 53
Bridget (daughter of Edward IV), 132
Bridgettines, Order of, 156
Brixius, Germanus (Germain de Brie), 91, 112, 142, 148, 157
Brooke, Serjeant Richard, 105
Bruges, 19–20, 101
Brussels, 107
Bryan. *See* Brian
Buckingham, Family of, 44, 98
Budé, Guillaume, 95, 112
Bullough, Geoffrey, 79
Burgundy, Ambassadors of, 107

Caesar, 77
Calais, 88–89, 92, 100–01, 104, 121
Cambrai, 102
Cambridge, University of, 20, 50, 108
Campbell, W. E., 50
Canterbury, 22, 156

Rogers, Elizabeth F., 9, 60, 80–81, 119–22, 152–57
Rolle, Richard, 12
Rome, 24, 29, 33, 40, 50–51, 55, 77, 88
Roper, John, 52
Roper, Margaret, 9, 52, 61, 63–67, 80, 132
Roper, William, 4–5, 7, 19, 44–46, 52–53, 55, 87, 91, 93, 96, 98, 101–02, 108, 111–12, 119–22, 130, 153
Ross, William (pseudonym of Thomas More), 112
Rotterdam, 137
Routh, E. M. G., 52, 112, 119–20, 122
Roy, William, 47
Russell, Sir John, 108
Ruthal, Thomas, Bishop of Durham, 135

Saint Asaph, 29
Saint Augustine, 13, 134, 138
Saint Bruno, 156
Saint Francis, 12, 146
Saint German, Christopher, 17, 23, 29, 34, 37–39, 44, 47, 50, 52–53, 55, 112
Saint Gregory, 156
Saint Jerome, 138
Saint John Chrysostom, 134
Saint John of the Cross, 152
Saint John the Baptist, 130
Saint John the Evangelist, 59
Saint Julian, 45
Saint Luke, 59, 128
Saint Margaret's, parish of, 53
Saint Mark, 59
Saint Mary's, parish of, 53
Saint Matthew, 59
Saint Paul, 71, 77, 145, 155
Saint Paul's Cathedral, 35
Saint Paul's Cross, 25, 27
Saint Peter, 45
Saint Veronica, 145

Sampson, Richard, 107, 136
Sandys, Sir William, 104
Savonarola, Girolamo, 157
Scarisbrick, J. J., 122
Schäfer, D., 54, 121
Schinner, Matthew, Cardinal of Sion, 104
Schoeck, R. J., 1–2, 4–6, 8–9, 15–55
Sejanus, 114
Sheehan, M. M., 52
Simpson, A. W. B., 51
Sion, Cardinal of. See Schinner, Matthew
Skelton, John, 17, 37
Smithfield, 25
Somerville, R., 120
Southampton, 19
South, Manor of, 98
Spain, 95, 101–02, 107
Spinelli, Sir Thomas, 88
Standish, Henry, 18, 26–29, 34–36, 39, 54
Stapleton, Thomas, 122, 146–47
Star Chamber, 19–20, 22, 93
Starkey, Thomas, 17
Steelyard, 111
Stoics, 155
Stokesley, John, 93
Stone, Walter, 31
Strasbourg, 50
Succession, Act of, 80
Succession, Oath of, 80
Supplication against the Ordinaries, 55
Supremacy, Act of, 17
Surtz, Edward, 2, 154
Sylvester, R. S., 2–14, 153, 158

Taft, A. I., 53, 158
Thompson, Craig, 12
Thrupp, Sylvia, 55
Toledo, 95
Tournay, Cathedral of, 136
Tower of London, 5, 7, 42, 59–62, 74–75, 139